LEGENDS OF THE AIR

LEGENDS OF THE AIR

AIRCRAFT, PILOTS, AND PLANEMAKERS FROM THE MUSEUM OF FLIGHT

BY SEAN ROSSITER

FOREWORD BY PETER M. BOWERS

SASQUATCH BOOKS
SEATTLE, WASHINGTON

p. 19: "Curtiss Jenny," by Peter Kilduff in *Flying the World's Great Aircraft*, ed. by Anthony Robinson, reprinted by permission of Orbis Publishing, Ltd.; p. 34: *Glacier Pilot: The Story of Bob Reeve and the Flyers Who Pushed Back Alaska's Air Frontiers*, by Beth Day, reprinted by permission of Henry Holt & Co.; p. 53: *Thunderbolt!* by Robert S. Johnson with Martin Caidin, reprinted with permission of Henry Holt & Co.; p. 68: *The Douglas DC-3*, by Len Morgan, reprinted with permission of TAB Books; p. 77: *The Fall of Fortresses*, by Elmer Bendiner, reprinted with permission of Elmer Bendiner; p. 85: *Samurai!* by Saburo Sakai with Martin Caidin and Fred Saito, reprinted by permission of Bantam Books, a division of Bantam Doubleday Dell, Inc.; p. 91: "Thoughts of a Combat Pilot," by Charles A. Lindbergh, reprinted from *The Saturday Evening Post* © 1954 The Curtis Publishing Co.; p. 94: *Flying the Old Planes*, by Frank Tallman, reprinted by permission of Doubleday, a division of Bantam Doubleday Dell, Inc.; p. 103: "Bomber 47," by Walter Boyne, reprinted by permission of *Wings*; p. 115: "Skyhawks for the Angels," by John Tegler, reprinted by permission of *Air Classics Quarterly Review*; p. 125: "Vought's Long-lived Photobird," by Peter Mersky, reprinted with the permission of Tri-Service Press; p. 136: *Carrying the Fire*, by Michael Collins, reprinted by permission of Farrar, Straus & Giroux; p. 135: "Lunar Reflections," © 1989 by Jeff Goldberg, reprinted by permission of Omni Publications International, Ltd.; p. 154: "VariViggen Designer Builder Report," by Burt Rutan, reprinted with permission of *Sport Aviation*.

Published by Sasquatch Books
1931 Second Avenue
Seattle, WA 98101
(206) 441-5555

Produced by Marquand Books, Inc.
Typeset by The Type Gallery, Inc., Seattle
Printed and bound in Japan by Toppan Printing Co., Ltd.
Cover: Curtiss Jenny

Library of Congress Cataloging-in-Publication Data

Rossiter, Sean, 1946-
    Legends of the air : aircraft, pilots, and planemakers from the Museum of Flight / by Sean Rossiter.
        p.   cm.
    Includes bibliographical references.
    ISBN 0-912365-31-5 : $35.00. — ISBN 0-912365-29-3 (pbk.) : $24.95
    1. Museum of Flight (Seattle, Wash.) 2. Airplanes — History.
I. Museum of Flight (Seattle, Wash.) II. Title.
TL506.U6S647   1990
629.13' 09 — dc20
                                                                        90-31010
                                                                        CIP

10 9 8 7 6 5 4 3 2 1

Contents

Foreword

The Museum of Flight, occupying the southwest corner of Seattle's Boeing Field, has been recognized as one of the world's major aviation museums since its Great Gallery opened to the public in July 1987. That such a museum came to be is due to the strong appreciation of aeronautical history on the part of the people of the Pacific Northwest and Alaska. While the Boeing Company has provided extensive support in the form of money, material, and services, to the point where some people refer to the Museum as "The Boeing Museum," such is definitely not the case. Company employees formed the backbone of the Museum's original organization, but the initiative for its founding was not provided by any corporation.

The activity that led to the establishment of the Museum began in 1960 in Alaska, when a Boeing Model 80A trimotor transport that had sat derelict at the Anchorage airport since the end of World War II was hauled to the nearby city dump. It was spotted there by Anchorage newspaperman Harriss Darby, who recognized the battered relic not only as the last of the biplane transports but as an airplane that had made airlift history during the war. He felt strongly that the plane, which he regarded as a jewel on the junkpile, should be saved. After some fast footwork, Darby beat the airplane's date with the bulldozer and obtained permission to move it to his property, where he stored it under cover with other antique airplanes he had acquired.

He then wrote to the public relations office of the Boeing Company in Seattle, telling of his acquisition and asking for photographs and drawings needed for the planned restoration. The request was forwarded to the late Harl V. Brackin Jr., then Boeing's Historical Services administrator, who rounded up the requested material.

A change of jobs made it impossible for Darby to undertake the restoration, so the 80A became available. Aviation museums as well as interested individuals wanted it, but all were stopped by the gigantic and costly task of moving the big airplane out of Alaska.

A Seattle-based airline pilot, Jack Leffler, acquired the 80A and was able to interest the Boeing Management Association (BMA, the "Supervisors' Club") in working out a way to return the plane to Seattle. Realizing that Boeing could not directly finance the task of transporting private property, BMA sought help from other organizations that would have an interest in seeing the old airliner returned to its birthplace.

Finally, a committee composed of BMA members backed by William M. Allen, then president of Boeing; Reno Odlin, president of the Washington State Historical Society; and Bruce Leroy, president of the Washington Historical Museum, prevailed upon Maj. Gen. H. R. Spicer at McChord Air Force Base in Tacoma, Washington, to airlift the dismantled 80A to the base on routine flights from Anchorage of the 62nd Troop Carrier's giant Douglas C-124A Globemaster cargo plane.

Spicer obtained approval from the Pentagon for the proposed airlift. The 80A arrived on two separate flights in February and March 1964 and was trucked to Plant 2 at Boeing Field.

The arrival of the relic in Seattle rallied many people, some of whom were members of the unofficial Seattle chapter of the American Aviation Historical Society. With Boeing unable to undertake refurbishment of the plane, the groups saw the need for an outside organization to do so. As a result, the Pacific Northwest Aviation Historical Foundation (PNAHF) was created. The old 80A airliner thereby became the artifact upon which PNAHF, since renamed the

Museum of Flight Foundation, was established. From twelve charter members in 1965, the foundation has grown to 12,000 members countrywide.

The project was moved into an unused West Coast Airlines hangar, where work proceeded as manpower and funds allowed. Later the old biplane was moved to a hangar at Sand Point Naval Air Station, north of Seattle, where restoration continued slowly.

Meanwhile, under the guidance of BMA, a proper organization for PNAHF was set up, with a board of trustees drawn largely from the Seattle business community. While some of the board members were pilots or were connected directly with aviation, most were not. However, all had a sincere appreciation of the significance of the Northwest's aviation heritage and the need to preserve it.

While it started small, PNAHF grew on sound corporate lines, impressing the aviation community. By 1967, enough aircraft and lesser artifacts had been donated or loaned to establish a small aviation museum in a rented building at the Seattle Center, the city's legacy from the 1962 World's Fair. Although repairs to the roof and upgrading of the heating system ate into PNAHF's meager funds, the museum, staffed entirely by volunteers, prospered.

It was known that the Seattle Center site was temporary, but the end came sooner than expected. The city announced that it had other uses for the building, and the museum closed in November 1977. This event speeded up plans that had been developing for a permanent aviation museum in a more appropriate location—Boeing Field.

A bold idea, considered by some at the time an impossible dream, was proposed by Harl Brackin. Boeing was in the process of selling to the Port of Seattle its abandoned Plant 1 site on the west side of the Duwamish River. The Port planned to raze the buildings and convert the land to a new shipping terminal. Plant 1 included the old "Red Barn," the original Heath Shipyard building that William E. Boeing

had acquired when he took over the small, financially troubled shipyard before World War I to ensure the completion of his yacht. The building became the first unit of the airplane manufacturing company that Boeing founded in July 1916, the Pacific Aero Products Company.

Brackin proposed to barge the complete building up the Duwamish from the Plant 1 site to Boeing Field, two miles upstream and across the river. Placed on a new foundation, refurbished, and stocked with artifacts, the historic building would make a fine aviation museum.

Not surprisingly, considering the dedication of the people involved, the dream came true. The Port saved the building from the wrecking ball and the Shaughnessy Company, a large Seattle house-moving firm, made the move.

The Red Barn is a building of great architectural significance in its own right, as one of the few surviving examples of a large all-wooden factory in the Northwest. Its restoration became the first phase of an even greater museum plan—the erection of a "Great Gallery" adjacent to the barn that would house a greater number of airplanes, many of them suspended from the ceiling.

The first phase was financed through an extensive local fund-raising campaign. To assist this drive, Boeing allowed its employees to be solicited through the company mail and to join PNAHF through payroll deductions. This effort raised nearly a million dollars, which the company matched with another million. The Seattle architectural firm of Ibsen Nelsen was engaged to put the Red Barn on new foundations and restore it. With a new coat of paint and the bright white lettering of its early days, the Red Barn was opened to the public as the Museum of Flight in September 1983.

The second phase then got under way with a financial target of $26.4 million for erection of the Great Gallery. T. A. Wilson, then-CEO of Boeing, headed the fund-raising committee and soon collected the required amount. Ibsen

Nelsen created a truly unique steel-and-glass building that was opened to the public in July 1987. The facility had an odd, federally mandated feature: because of its proximity to the Boeing Field runway, the building had to comply with Federal Aviation Administration requirements concerning building height relative to distance from the runway. The roof of the Great Gallery slopes eastward toward the runway in order to fit under the inner limits of this height/distance envelope.

While construction was going on, the Museum Foundation continued to acquire significant historical material, which now numbers some 155,000 items, including seventy complete aircraft. Since those cannot all be displayed at Boeing Field, a branch museum is being established at Paine Field, in Everett, Washington. In this volume, Sean Rossiter describes what he considers to be twenty-two of the most important commercial, military, and homebuilt aircraft in the Museum's collection. His presentations are not mere catalog descriptions of inanimate hardware. He has researched the histories of these aircraft from their design process to their first flights. He tells how they were developed and how they were used, and he writes about the people who built and flew them.

It is hoped that this volume will increase your appreciation both of these particular planes (and one spacecraft) and of the goals of the museum, which was founded for scientific and educational purposes, to foster and sponsor research and writing on aeronautical and aerospace subjects, and to collect and display artifacts for experts and the general public alike.

Peter M. Bowers
December 1989

Preface

Flying machines of all kinds are the most fascinating artifacts of the twentieth century. Like any other products of civilization they have been designed, built, and used by people. Yet the history of these machines is often told with a curious absence of human characters. The stories of such intriguing pioneers of aviation as the speed demon Glenn Curtiss; the quiet, almost reclusive Leroy Grumman; and William E. Boeing, who built a nationwide industrial empire on good ideas and great talent, have seldom appeared in aviation books for the general reader.

I have attempted in this book to show how milestone aircraft from Seattle's Museum of Flight were designed, built, and flown by men and women with their own talents and dreams. Many of those profiled in these pages are or were geniuses, with all the eccentricities and all-too-human quirks that accompany brilliant minds. Like all of us, they were products of their times, shaped by their own successes and failures.

The Museum of Flight exhibits a range of aircraft that illustrates how aeronautical engineering has evolved in the United States. Eighteen commercial and military planes appear in this book, from the only mass-produced American airplane of World War I, the Curtiss JN-4D Jenny, to an early example of the Apollo spacecraft that took three Americans to the moon. These are supplemented by four homebuilt airplanes included as a tribute to the skill, ingenuity, and hard work of hundreds of people who have constructed their own aircraft.

It makes sense to publish this personal approach to the history of American aircraft engineering in Seattle, where tens of thousands of people have spent their lifetimes in the production of the most successful, continuous line of civil and military aircraft in the world. Seattle is one of the few communities left whose lifeblood is airplanes; the city has become an aviation capital through the Boeing Company's careful balance of innovation, consistent craftsmanship, and market savvy. In Seattle, the people who build airplanes have names—many of them appear in this book.

In particular, the six Boeing designs chosen from the Museum's collection, from the 80A to the 747, demonstrate how the Boeing Company emerged from building stick-and-wire derivatives of other companies' designs to worldwide leadership in aeronautics at the hands of such men as C. N. "Monty" Montieth and Edward C. Wells. That such a young collection as the Museum of Flight's can so clearly illustrate the development of American aeronautical engineering is testimony to the dedication of the Museum's curators, under the leadership of Victor Seely, and the generosity of dozens of donors, many of them prominent in Seattle's sophisticated aviation culture.

All of the Museum's holdings could not be presented in this single volume. And some of the aircraft included here were not on display at the Museum itself as of January 1990: the Boeing 247D, the 747 prototype, and the FM-2 Wildcat were at the Museum's restoration facility at Everett's Paine Field; the Rutan VariViggen was at another museum; and the Lear Fan was on exhibit at Seattle-Tacoma International Airport. Of the aircraft on exhibit, the B-17F is on loan to the Museum, which is raising money for its purchase, and appears courtesy of its owner, Bob Richardson. The XF8U-1 Crusader prototype appears courtesy of the National Air and Space Museum, Washington, D.C.

A number of people have made extraordinary contributions to the research and collection of materials for this book. First among the unsung heroes of any book project is its editor, but in this case Anne Depue of Sasquatch Books can more accurately be credited with being the producer of *Legends of the Air.* Barry Foy, from the outset a meticulous guardian of proper English usage, soon became an enthusiastic student of the more arcane aspects of aviation terminology.

It is one thing for an institution such as the Museum of Flight to give its blessing to an undertaking like this one; it is another for the archivist to have to deliver the goods. Anne Rutledge did so single-handedly and with remarkably good cheer. Howard Fox, keeper of the Seattle Public Library's Aero Room, took an immediate and lasting interest in this project, often anticipating my needs, and I thank him. Boeing's Marilyn Phipps, perhaps the most acknowledged airplane company archivist in the United States, made material contributions to my knowledge of the little-known chief engineers of the Boeing Company. Matt Fikse was the Museum's earliest supporter of this project and was there during the last-minute crunch. He brought his extensive knowledge of the space program to bear on the spacecraft chapter and in the process made me an ardent convert to the poetry of the subject.

I was an admirer of Peter M. Bowers, wartime B-17 engineering officer, pilot and aircraft designer, historian and photo-archivist, long before this book was conceived. His thorough fact-checking and gentle critiques at each stage of the book's preparation amounted to a priceless education. Dozens of rare photographs from his personal collection have enlivened this book. For the Hiller YH-32 chapter, Jay P. Spenser's generous sharing of insights from interviews for his forthcoming volume on the life and work of Stanley Hiller Jr. was especially helpful. Their reviews of the manuscript saved me countless embarrassments, although they can neither guarantee the accuracy of this volume, nor can they necessarily agree with its conclusions. For errors of fact or interpretation, I am solely responsible.

Curtiss Jenny

"If you can fly a Jenny, you can fly anything."

In the first years of this century the United States was home to the leading pioneers in aviation. In August 1908, Wilbur Wright demonstrated for France the Wright Flyer, an improved version of the world's first powered flying machine. After Wright's perfectly controlled flight, French aviator René Gasnier declared, "We are as children compared with the Wrights." One year later at Reims, New Yorker Glenn Curtiss won the first air race ever, beating Louis Blériot in a specially built racer he constructed in less than a month. His speed record: 43.35 miles per hour.

But by the outbreak of World War I, leadership in flight technology had passed to the Europeans, who had started the airplane on its way to becoming an instrument of mass destruction. How far behind the United States had fallen was shown by the nation's main contribution to the war effort in the air, the Curtiss JN-4D "Jenny." It was nowhere near equal to the combat aircraft in action over Europe, even though it proved an overachiever on the home front.

Like early twentieth-century America, the Curtiss Jenny was a composite, assembled from many sources. Designed by an Englishman, B. Douglas Thomas, it flew best with Swiss-designed, Spanish-engineered Hispano-Suiza engines. A little less than half the Jennys built were manufactured in Canada, many of them for the British Royal Flying Corps (RFC). Conceived as a combination of the better features from Curtiss's earlier J and N models, even the Jenny's name was a hybrid, a corruption of the model designation JN.

Almost a Jenny: a JN-3 built
for Britain, with deliveries
beginning March 1915.

An Army lieutenant crashed this Jenny while on an unauthorized flight with his girlfriend in 1918 — no small accomplishment, considering the scarcity of trees in the area. Both survived.

There were dozens of versions of the plane in service. The Jenny, by trade a single-engined two-seat trainer, was turned into whatever the U.S. Army Air Service required — even a twin-engined bomber. The old joke "a bunch of parts flying in formation" was never more aptly applied than to the Jenny.

Its achievements far surpassed its humble origins. More than ninety percent of North American World War I combat pilots learned to fly in Curtiss Jennys. Wartime conditions made it a priority to turn out 6,070 of them, an impressive total by any standard. After the war, the plane's easy availability for as little as a couple of hundred dollars made it an airmail trailblazer and the choice of the barnstorming legions who introduced rural America to powered flight during the 1920s.

The Jenny was legislated out of commercial service in 1927 by new airworthiness regulations that rendered it instantly obsolete. Over a dozen survive, with eight flyable.

The Museum of Flight's Jenny is considered one of the finest examples left in the world: the exquisite craftsmanship that has gone into its restoration justifies leaving the skin off the airplane, as a three-dimensional cutaway demonstration of how aircraft were built in those days of stick, wire, and fabric.

The Jenny story begins with the engines that were Glenn Curtiss's first claim to fame. Most of his early designs were powered by his own water-cooled, 26- to 90-horsepower V-8 engine, mounted behind the pilot and driving a propeller that pushed the aircraft rather than pulling it. The Curtiss Pusher of 1909–11, powered by the Curtiss V-8, was the standard American aircraft design before World War I. Eugene Ely pioneered carrier aviation by taking off in a Pusher from a deck built on the cruiser *Birmingham* at Norfolk, Virginia, on November 14, 1910. The end for the Pushers came in early 1914 when they were grounded: the rear-mounted engine tended to come loose in crashes and kill pilots who might otherwise have survived. The government asked Curtiss for a "tractor" airplane, that is, with the engine and propeller in front.

The Museum of Flight's JN-4D Jenny was rebuilt in the wood shop of Paul Whittier, in Washington's San Juan Islands.

Curtiss's Model J of early 1914 was a clean, functional design. Thomas, its designer, had worked for the English Sopwith and Avro companies, and the Model J and subsequent N looked similar to earlier Avro designs. Those similarities made the Curtiss Model JN attractive to the RFC. The Model J had equal-span wings, soon modified to add area by lengthening the upper wings through the addition of the distinctive overwing king-post brackets, one of the Jenny's notable features.

The RFC bought some JN-2s and JN-3s in 1915–17 for primary training. To ensure an immediate supply at a time

PLANEMAKER:
GLENN HAMMOND CURTISS

Glenn H. Curtiss was a speed maniac who became the world's fastest human in 1907 by doing 136mph on a motorcycle with an engine of his own design. Soon he was looking for ways of going higher and faster. Photographs of him show an intense, unsmiling pure competitor who spoke readily of "my craving for speed."

Like his archrivals, the Wright brothers, Curtiss built bicycles before he got off the ground. But Curtiss took up development of the airplane where the Wrights left off. After designing and building dozens of types of seaplanes and land-based aircraft from 1909 to 1915, he was the only contractor ready to build airplanes by the thousands for the United States' war effort. The airplane he built was the Jenny.

Eventually—long after Curtiss and Orville, the surviving Wright brother, had left the airplane business—decades of court battles over airplane patents were settled, and the two sides' manufacturing interests were merged in 1929 to form the mighty Curtiss-Wright Aeronautical Corporation, the biggest combined aero-engine and airframe manufacturer in America prior to World War II.

Born in Hammondsport, in upstate New York, on May 21, 1878, young Glenn showed all the earmarks of a future inventor. Whatever he needed, he invented: a kitelike sail to improve his ice skating, a crude form of telegraph, and cameras (after working for a short time at the Eastman Kodak factory at Rochester). In 1901, three years after starting work in a bicycle repair shop, he started his own bicycle factory. Soon he was designing and building motorcycles. In 1904 he supplied the engine for the balloon that made the first circular flight in America. The balloon's designer, Thomas Scott Baldwin, joined Curtiss at Hammondsport in 1906.

By 1906, all airships in the United States were reported to have been powered by Curtiss engines (an assertion difficult to confirm today). The first aircraft purchased by the U.S. Army was a Baldwin dirigible powered by a Curtiss air-cooled engine in 1908. Price: $6,740.

Meanwhile, Curtiss was moving to the forefront of heavier-than-air design. The quality of his engines led to his being invited to join Alexander Graham Bell's Aerial Experiment Association in late 1907. He was named Director of Experiments. The association produced four airplanes, the third of which was Curtiss's design, the *June Bug*. It flew on June 21, 1908, and won Curtiss his first Scientific American Trophy for flying more than one kilometer on the Fourth of July that year. Less than a month later Curtiss and Baldwin sold their airship to the Army.

In 1909 Curtiss set a world air speed record of 47.6mph. In May 1910 he won *The New York World*'s $10,000 prize (and the Scientific American trophy for a third time, giving him permanent possession) for the first flight from Albany to New York City, accomplished at an average speed of 54.8mph, in a development of the *June Bug*, the *Hudson Flyer*. *The New York Times* devoted eight pages to the accomplishment. Curtiss was the first winner of the Collier Trophy, awarded by the president of the United States, in 1911 for his invention of the float-equipped seaplane, and again in 1913 for the flying boat, with its integral boat-hulled fuselage.

It was to design the wing for his biggest flying boat to date, the Model H America of 1913, that Curtiss first employed B. Douglas Thomas, the English Sopwith Aviation Company engineer who later designed the Jenny. The Curtiss company's designs were soon to include the NC-4 (for "Navy Curtiss Number 4") flying boats that crossed the Atlantic for the first time in May 1919.

Curtiss's Jenny was far from state-of-the-art in 1916, but it capitalized on America's industrial capacity, appearing in vast numbers to train pilots for the European war. It became the foundation for the Curtiss-Wright empire, which Glenn Curtiss left in 1921 to make far more money promoting Florida real estate. He died in 1930. By then, the plane that put America into the air was outlawed, a quickly fading memory and legend in the making.

when the United States was still neutral, the Crown purchased the former Curtiss factory in Toronto, renamed it Canadian Aeroplanes Ltd., and set up production there of a JN-3 revamped by John Ericson, the JN-4 model. This Canadian version of the Jenny was called the Canuck and was similar to the JN-4D evolving at the same time in the United States. It had a control stick instead of the JN-3's wheel, metal tube-framed tail components instead of wood, and four ailerons, one for each wing panel. (American-built Jennys soon incorporated many of these changes but had ailerons only in the upper wings.) Canucks were therefore somewhat more responsive, and highly prized by postwar barnstormers.

Canadian production quickly peaked at 350 for the month of February 1917, and enough airframes for a total of 2,900, worth $14 million (U.S.), were built there. Whole stands of timber on the British Columbia coast were bought for building Canucks. When the supply of Irish linen for covering their wings was interrupted by U-boats, milled cotton was brought in from Quebec. OX-5 engines came from the United States, the best ones from Hammondsport, New York, but the majority from various American automobile manufacturers. With Canadian production well under way, Curtiss began production in earnest at its new Buffalo plant. Jennys were also built by subcontractors in eight additional cities.

No aircraft is better than the engine that powers it. The OX-5 was a good engine for its time. At Reims the Curtiss water-cooled V-8 had astonished the French. By the 1920s, one old-timer was calling his OX-5 "Galloping Dominoes," because if he didn't have an engine failure in seven hours, he would have one in eleven.

Installing the 150hp Hispano-Suiza engine made all the difference, offering nearly double the horsepower for an additional 15 pounds of weight. "Hisso" Jennys climbed faster, had almost twice the ceiling, and offered 20mph more speed. Most of these more powerful JN-4H Jennys were kept by the Air Service after the war.

The Jenny's vices became virtues for the barnstormers. An OX-5 Jenny could be had for as little as $500 to $1,000 — some changed hands during the mid-twenties, with the airplane's twilight in sight, for fifty dollars. The OX-5 was easy to fix in a pasture. The wire-braced king posts above the wings were a wingwalker's salvation: footholds and handrails. Curved skids under the lower wing, designed to save the lower wingtips from destruction at the hands of ground-looping student pilots, enabled adventurous blondes to hang from underneath.

Legend traces the origins of wingwalking to Ormer Locklear, a Texan who found himself training to be a Signal Corps flying officer in 1917. The story goes that he threw a trailing radio antenna out of his Jenny only to have it snag in the external tail-control wires. So he climbed out of the cockpit and made his way along the turtleback, untangling the antenna just in time to receive the message "Locklear, U R grounded."

Movie stunt pilot Frank Tallman tells the story of test-flying a Jenny he had just bought in St. Louis during the 1950s. It had a modern Ranger engine that enabled him to climb to 8,000 feet, an altitude no OX-5-powered Jenny could have attained.

Captain Benjamin Foulois, the first U.S. Army aviator, with his JN-2, converted here to a JN-3, 1916.

One Bad Move

Following his discharge from the Royal Air Force in 1920, Carl Dixon flew with the Ivan R. Gates Air Circus, one of the more successful traveling aviation exhibitions of the barnstorming period. He vividly recalled one of the highlights of the show, the wing walkers:

When I first joined the air circus the chief stuntman asked me if I had ever walked out on the wing of an aeroplane. I said, "Hell no, and I don't intend to, either." Then he asked if I would fly a plane in which a man would walk from its wings to a plane flying alongside. I told him, "If the guy is crazy enough to pull a stunt like that, I'll fly him anywhere he wants to go."

As it turned out, the chief stuntman, a guy named Bartlett, was my passenger during the next air show. He explained that he would leave the cockpit, walk out on the bottom wing, climb up the struts to the top wing and then walk between the top bracing wires and the kingposts all along the length of the top wing and over to the bottom wing of another aeroplane.

You could do a stunt like that in a Jenny, because it was big enough and a very stable aeroplane. The tricky part was keeping the aeroplane on an even keel. As I felt Bartlett walk across the top wing, from left to right, I had to compensate gradually, tilting slightly to the right until he got to the middle of the wing. Then I'd tilt more to the left so he had an even platform as he continued his walk. Bartlett wore no parachute, so one bad move would have been the end of him. But the toughest part was when he got ready to move over to the other aeroplane. At exactly the right moment I had to be ready to turn into the other plane, since the loss of the wing walker's weight would naturally cause the wing to "lift" up and probably knock him off the other aeroplane. At the same time, the other pilot had to be prepared for the additional weight about to be on his left wingtip.

The first time I tried to fly Bartlett, I pulled away a second too soon, to keep from hitting the other aeroplane, and poor Bartlett was hanging in mid-air, with only one hand on a strut of the other plane. Fortunately, he was a very muscular guy and could pull himself up. But, when we got back on the ground, he chewed my tail off for almost dumping him. It was a crazy way to make a living....

—Peter Kilduff, "Curtiss Jenny," in *Flying the World's Great Aircraft*, edited by Anthony Robinson

Facing page: Ormer Locklear performs a midair inspection of the Jenny's struts and wires on a flight over Los Angeles; *inset*: These wings were made for walkin'. The king posts above the wing and the wingtip skids below were there for structural and safety reasons, but they also allowed daredevil stunts. *This page*: Gladys Ingle demonstrates a quick flight connection. In the first photo, the pilot of the oncoming aircraft is lowering his left wing—note the raised aileron. As Ingle climbs aboard, the left aileron is already down and the wingtip is rising to compensate for her weight.

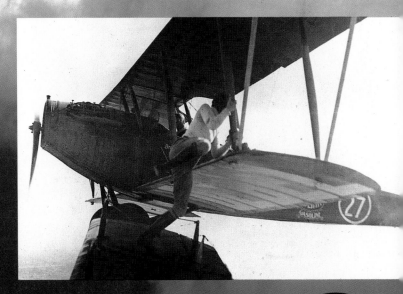

Up there, "looking out at the exposed elevator [control wires] and flapping aileron wires, I hoped that in World War I everyone did nice wing work, because it is amazing how much higher eight thousand feet looks than five hundred or a thousand feet."

Suddenly, Tallman found himself being buzzed from behind by a Lockheed Constellation, the biggest intercontinental airliner of the time. To slow to the Jenny's speed, it dropped its landing gear and huge Fowler flaps, and drifted in a lazy circle around him and his ancient-looking kite. Passengers waved from the dozens of windows, and, Tallman writes, "I felt as exposed as a man taking a shower in Central Park. With a parting flirt of its three tails, the Connie departed, and I was left alone in fifteen-degree cold...."

A Jenny's cockpit as it looked to the pilot.

CURTISS JN-4D JENNY

Dimensions

Overall wingspan .... 43ft 7^3/$_8$in

Overall length 27ft 4in

Height .... 9ft 10^5/$_8$in

Engine

Curtiss OX-5 water-cooled V-8, 90hp

Weight

Empty 1,390lbs

Loaded 1,920lbs

Performance

Maximum speed 75mph

Cruise 60mph

Endurance 2hrs 18min

Boeing P-12

The Boeing P-12 was the definitive American fighter plane of the 1930s, the golden age of aviation. Its chunky profile, from the big, flat, reliable air-cooled radial engine to the broad tail surfaces, set the pattern for American pursuit planes until well into World War II. The P-12 became stockier as it developed, sturdy rather than fast and easy rather than tricky to fly. It was a commercial success but not a milestone of aerodynamic design. Although P-12s were often decorated with the flashy stripes and colorful heraldry of the peacetime military, the airplane was anything but flamboyant.

The P-12 was the frontline pursuit plane of both the U.S. Navy and the Army Air Corps through the early 1930s. The prototype, designed to meet a Navy requirement, was developed from a series of Navy carrier fighters that dated back to 1925. The Army monitored the Navy's tests of the new F4B, liked it, and immediately ordered ten equivalent P-12s. (For information on the designations given to Army and Navy airplane types, see sidebar.) These were far more maneuverable than the Curtiss pursuits then in service. Some civil versions of the plane (Model 100) were developed into potent racers and stunt planes by such notable pilots as Milo Burcham and Howard Hughes.

A total of 586 of the P-12/F4B/Model 100 series were built from 1928 to 1933, a remarkable production run during the Depression. The P-12 made the Boeing Company America's foremost fighter-plane supplier at a time when many companies were struggling to stay in business.

The main P-12 innovation was the use of bolted aluminum tubing in its fuselage structure in place of welded steel tubing. Beginning with Model E, this frame was covered entirely with sheet aluminum, making it stronger but lighter than earlier steel-and-fabric designs. As a result the P-12 could withstand higher G-loads in aerial maneuvers, and offered better engine vibration damping and improved protection for the pilot from gunfire or crashes.

Later models featured an engine cowling ring, a streamlined removable cover that greatly smoothed airflow over the bulky radial engines. (The Museum of Flight P-12 is one of the very rare earlier models without the cowling.) The series was developed through no fewer than ten models.

The P-12 was surprisingly influential—chiefly because of its sheer conventionality—and both the Soviet Union and Japan built derivatives. A Chinese P-12 was the first fighter to shoot down a Japanese aircraft in the Sino-Japanese conflict, downing two of its attackers before itself being destroyed by the third. Army P-12s had been replaced by P-26 monoplanes in frontline service by 1935, but the Navy's F4Bs soldiered on until 1938 because of their excellent maneuverability, low landing approach speeds, and resistance to the heavy wear of carrier operations. Both

Above: P-12Bs in formation, 1930. *Above right*: Boeing test pilot Lew Wallick takes the newly restored Museum of Flight P-12 up for its second maiden flight. *Facing page*: U.S. Navy F4B-3s.

She Quit Cold

Rigged for inverted flight, etc., he was exquisitely smooth and precise with the airplane. Most of the show was with the airplane seldom right side up. With its tremendous power, he put on a better show with greater performance upside down than contemporary airplanes could manage right side up most of the time. But I saw him almost bust his tail with it as he started to fly a session for news photos the day before his scheduled show.

There was a belly tank between the landing gears for inverted flight that he either neglected to fill, or it fed improperly. In any case, he rolled inverted right after lift-off and started a steep climb—and, boy, would it go up! Well, she quit cold at a few hundred feet and he went out of sight behind trees at the edge of the airport in about a 40-degree bank still rolling toward level as the engine spluttered back to life. Everyone thought he had had it, but the airplane somehow reappeared and came up out of there flying. That ended the "press show" and he tip-toed around and landed and taxied up to the ramp where he shut her down. He then sat there all by himself with helmet strapped and goggles still down for a good half-hour.

—Captain "Dutch" Redfield, retired Pan American training captain, recalling Milo Burcham's air show in Syracuse, New York

The devil in disguise: The Museum of Flight's P-12 rebuilt as a two-seat Curtiss F8C-2 Helldiver for the movie *Task Force,* co-starring Gary Cooper.

types were still in second-line service after Pearl Harbor.

The first Army P-12, the *Pan American*, was flown to Central America on a speed-flight goodwill mission by Capt. Ira C. Eaker in 1929. Nearly ten years later, Eaker completed the first transcontinental instrument flight in a P-12, flying all the way under a specially designed blind-flying hood. Eaker later became Commanding General of the U.S. Army Air Force Eighth Air Force in England.

Most of the surviving P-12/F4B airplanes were assigned to the Navy in 1941 for use as target drones. The handful of present-day survivors were either assigned as ground crew training aids or used by civilian air-show performers.

The Museum of Flight's P-12 is the second of eight single-seat civil Boeing Model 100s built along with the military ones (plus an additional 100A two-seater). The first Model 100, which flew October 8, 1929, was bought by what is now the Federal Aviation Administration. The second, the Museum of Flight's aircraft, serial number 1143, was sold that year to the aero-engine manufacturer Pratt & Whitney as an engine test bed. It was equipped with a quick-change engine mount and is reported to have flown with three different P&W engines in one day to demonstrate its versatility. The third was retained by Boeing as a test aircraft and later sold to the movie stunt pilot Paul Mantz, who at one time owned both it and the Museum of Flight aircraft. The fourth 100 was sold to Japan. Two more 100s, designated Model 100E, were exported to Thailand, where one survives in the Thai Air Force Museum, in Bangkok, and the eighth was another engine test bed for Pratt & Whitney.

The one and only two-seat 100A was modified for racing by the young Howard Hughes. Hughes, it seems, was not taken seriously as an airman until he won a sportsman pilot's air race over Miami in the 100A in 1930. Later on, decked out with rakish streamlined wheel spats, a deeper cowl, and a taller fin, the Hughes plane had a 30-year career as an air-show performer, being flown by Col. Art Goebel and a succession of others until 1957, when it was destroyed.

After its career with Pratt & Whitney, the Museum of Flight's aircraft was sold to Milo Burcham on September 27, 1933. He modified it for skywriting and air-show work, painted it blood red, added fuel and oil systems for inverted flight, and flew it upside down from Los Angeles to San Diego. In 1936 he won the World Aerobatic Championship at the Los Angeles National Air Races in it, beating specially designed European stunt planes and their government-supported pilots.

Number 1143 was also a movie star. It appeared in *Men with Wings* in 1938 and in an early 1940s movie, title unknown, in which it was disguised as a British Gloster Gladiator fighter. It may have been damaged at that time. Mantz bought it for spare parts in 1948 (ten years after Burcham had sold it) and reassembled it to look like a two-seat Curtiss F8C-2 Helldiver for the film *Task Force*. (Mantz, by the way, became known as "Mr. Upside Down" by flying inverted in the third Model 100, the next one off the Boeing line, in a wheel-to-wheel air-show stunt with Frank Clarke.)

The Museum of Flight's airplane has been restored as an early P-12, a representation made easy by the fact that the sole difference between the military P-12 and the Model 100 was the lack of armament on the civil version. The Model 100's reduced weight made it faster than the military P-12/F4B, nudging some of the 100s close to the 200-mile-per-hour range.

This aircraft was discovered as a basket case in Florida by Seattle attorney Robert S. Mucklestone, who bought it in early 1977 in partnership with Boeing chief of test flight S. L. "Lew" Wallick. Orville Tosch headed the restoration team. The machine guns that would have armed a P-12 have been simulated on the Museum's aircraft, and it bears the "Kicking Mule" insignia of the famed 95th Pursuit Squadron, based during the early 1930s at March Field, near Riverside, California.

Lew Wallick takes off from Boeing Field in the oldest airworthy Boeing airplane. *Left*: A spiffy Howard Hughes, circa 1930, with his extensively modified supercharged racing Boeing 100A. It reportedly could do 225mph.

Three Boeing P-12s of the
95th Pursuit Squadron, front,
with older Boeing PW-9Ds
behind.

MILITARY AIRCRAFT TAGS

During the early 1920s, the U.S. Army Air Service and U.S. Navy adopted separate systems for designating their aircraft types. The Army's designations explained a particular type's role (such as P for pursuit, the Army's term for a fighter), its numerical rank in the sequence of such aircraft, and the model within that specific type's development. For example, the Boeing P-12 was the twelfth pursuit type ordered since the series began in 1924. Most P-12s had a letter added to denote their stage in the model's evolution, for example, P-12A and P-12B.

The Navy's system emphasized the aircraft's purpose and manufacturer. The P-12 was known to the Navy as the F4B type (F meant fighter, 4 indicated the fourth of its type ordered from Boeing, whose Navy code letter was B). Developmental stages were denoted by a number added to the designation, such as in F4B-1 and F4B-2. The first Navy aircraft carrier, the USS *Langley,* was commissioned on March 20, 1922.

Both services have used an X prefix to denote experimental aircraft, usually prototypes. The Army used the letter Y to indicate Service Test status (flown under actual field conditions), as with the seven YP-12Ks, which were P-12Es tested with fuel-injection systems.

Before either service designated them, the two P-12/F4B prototypes had been numbered Models 83 and 89 in Boeing's sequential model system. The main difference between the two was Model 89's lack of a cross-axle between the wheels, which allowed it to carry a 500-pound bomb on its longitudinal center of gravity. There was no XF4B prototype; Boeing simply presented Models 83 and 89 for testing and allowed the Navy to take its choice. Both prototypes were bought by the Navy and assigned the first two serial numbers of the F4B-1 contract.

BOEING P-12E/F4B-3 MODELS

Dimensions

Overall wingspan 30ft

Overall length 20ft 4in

Height 8ft 9in

Engine

Pratt & Whitney "E" Series Wasp, 500hp

at 200rpm at 6,000ft

Weight

Empty 1,981lbs

Loaded 2,674lbs

Performance

Maximum speed 190mph

Cruise 167mph

Range 475mi

Lineup of P-12Ds at March Field, California, home of the
34th Pursuit Squadron.

INSPECTION BOX NACELLE

793K
BOEING

The Model 80A, "Pullman of the Air," carried 18 passengers and established 27-hour coast-to-coast service. The fuselage was welded steel tubing, with steel wing spars and dural ribs, all fabric covered. *Inset*: Building the Boeing 80As, November 1929.

Boeing 80A

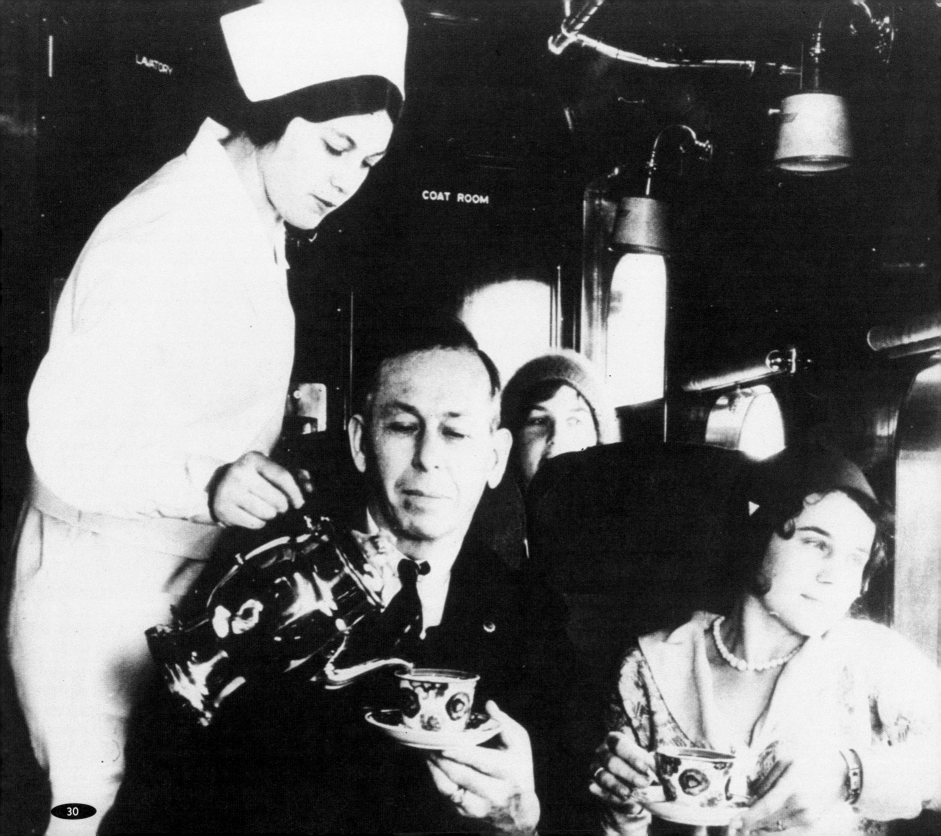

During the late 1920s, when the first monoplane airliners were already in service, the introduction of a trimotored biplane that cruised at a leisurely 120 miles per hour appeared to be a step backward. Two wings, three engines, three rudders, forests of struts and wires: the Boeing Model 80 drifted through the clouds like some windjammer of the trade winds.

From the inside—the passenger's point of view—the Model 80 was a step toward the future. It was downright luxurious, considering that most pilots of the day sat outdoors and their passengers either shivered in the other cockpit or huddled in the mail compartment. The Boeing—the very name was briefly a generic term for comfort aloft—introduced soundproofing, individual reading lights and air vents, cabin heating, Honduras mahogany paneling, a toilet with hot and cold running water, and flight instruments mounted on the forward bulkhead for the benefit of the dozen passengers, along with a map of the route.

For all that, the Boeing 80's place in commercial aviation history is secured by the fact it was the first multiengine airliner built by the company that now dominates the commercial transport industry. Not to mention that its immediate successor, Model 80A, gave a world of lonely travelers its first flight attendants.

The generous wing area above and below the large windows was reassuring to the adventurers stepping aboard for the type's maiden flight with Boeing Air Transport (BAT) from Salt Lake City to Cheyenne in August 1928. The biplane configuration, which offered oodles of lift, was specifically tailored to the mountainous terrain covered by BAT's first routes.

The Boeing 80 was rushed into service to take advantage of a gold mine in air passenger travel that Boeing stumbled upon while delivering airmail: two people would pay

Facing page: The friendlier skies: Boeing Air Transport employed the first flight attendants, all qualified nurses, aboard its Model 80A airliners in 1930. *Above*: Model 80s under construction, Boeing Plant 1, July 7, 1928.

Monty Montieth, leaning on the wing of a Boeing 247, explains a set of engineering drawings to a production supervisor. *Facing page*: Willing hands and a strong back: Away from the drawing board, former halfback Monty Montieth unloads the front mail compartment of a Boeing 40A.

DESIGNER:
C.N. "MONTY" MONTIETH

Charles N. "Monty" Montieth was Boeing's first nationally recognized chief engineer. A big man in stature, he was a larger-than-life character in other ways as well: he played halfback at Washington University in St. Louis, became a World War I pilot and flying instructor, and graduated in engineering from the Massachusetts Institute of Technology after the war. He could draw and paint, play several musical instruments, and was considered an expert photographer.

In 1922 Montieth was an Army Air Service procurement officer at McCook Field in Dayton, Ohio. A number of America's outstanding early aero-engineering minds were there at the time, including Maj. Reuben Fleet, the future founder of Consolidated Aircraft. Montieth may have been the best of a talented lot, having become chief of the Airplane Section of McCook's Engineering Division two years after leaving Massachusetts Institute of Technology. He had written the Army's standard textbook on aeronautical engineering, *Simple Aerodynamics and the Airplane*. He also spent three years on the aerodynamics subcommittee of the National Advisory Committee for Aeronautics.

His rapid rise continued after he came to work for Boeing in 1925. He was chief engineer by 1927 and a vice president in 1934.

Montieth designed two important Boeing types: the Boeing 80 in late 1927 and the P-26A fighter in late 1931. Both were characteristic of Montieth's design philosophy, i.e., strong, conservative, safe. Although the P-26A was the first monoplane fighter to enter service in the United States, it also had such dated features as wire-braced wings, an open cockpit, and fixed, spatted landing gear. Montieth had watched a buddy die at Kelly Field, Texas, when the wings sheared off his trainer, and the experience had made him wary of innovation.

Younger engineers, headed by Bob Minshall, designed the Model 200 Monomail, Boeing's first truly innovative design. At Montieth's insistence, it was laid out in both monoplane and biplane forms until the advantages of the monoplane's reduced drag became obvious to both teams.

Montieth was visibly horrified to see a veteran airmail pilot named Slim Lewis loop the Monomail three consecutive times for the sheer joy of it during an early flight test. Harold Mansfield describes Montieth waving his fists at the sky in frustration. Aside from popping some wing-root rivets, the Monomail suffered no structural damage, much to Montieth's surprise. He also had his reservations about the experimental variable-pitch propeller that Hamilton Standard tested on the Monomail to help take advantage of its aerodynamic slickness.

In 1932 Montieth was still insisting on alternative biplane or braced high-wing configuration schemes for what became the first American low-wing monoplane airliner, the Boeing 247. Later, he found the big wing flaps young Ed Wells was designing for the B-17 awfully daring and suggested he leave them off. Monty Montieth, the avuncular, pipe-smoking Renaissance man, found himself being left behind by the breathtaking pace of aviation progress during the mid-thirties.

Yet it was Montieth who had recruited and developed the generation of engineers who took Boeing to the forefront of four-engine airplane development. His was a consistent voice for safety in a company whose name was becoming synonymous with safe airplanes.

Montieth was forced to retire from Boeing in 1938 because of failing eyesight. Despondent, according to his wife, at the prospect of going blind, the consequence of the strain of writing his textbook on aeronautics, Montieth shot himself on March 17, 1940. He was forty-eight.

UNLOADING CARGO
FROM FRONT COMPARTMEN
BOEING M   PLANE

1513

Alaskan Repairs

Bob Reeve's past was, if anything, more colorful than his yellow Boeing 80's. He lied his way into the Army in 1917 at the age of fifteen; hopped a slow boat to China in 1919; was expelled from the University of Wisconsin for cutting classes to fool around in a Curtiss Jenny; was discharged from the Army Air Corps for high blood pressure; and pioneered airmail over the Andes in Ford Tri-Motors. He appeared in *Ripley's Believe It or Not* for flying blind in a blizzard through the Upsallata Pass without knowing it. After dropping $17,000 in the stock market in 1932, Reeve arrived in Alaska as a stowaway.

*Once [Reeve] made a landing in a bad crosswind, and the motor mount broke on his right engine. With no welding equipment available, and no time for repairs anyhow, Bob simply took a log chain and secured the motor mount to the pedestal by weaving the heavy chain in and out. But with every take-off and landing the chain stretched a little, and the engine became shaky.... He put bolts in the chain links around the mount, and after every trip he tightened the bolts, making the chain taut again. To expedite this six-times-daily tightening, he left the cowling off the engine mount. The Yellow Peril, with her cowling off and a log chain around her neck, looked somewhat like a lady caught with her slip show-*ing. As he was loading one day, Reeve heard a plane flying over, about to land. Thinking it an Army bomber on a practice run, he looked up casually, saw CAA in wide letters under the wing.

"Mindful of my past experiences with [the Civil Aeronautics Authority's] Hugh Brewster and Charley Burnett, who evidenced a lack of sympathy at some forms of 'Alaskan repair,' I yelled, 'Quick, shut off that loading. We got to get out of here before they see this engine!'"

Reeve hastily flew over to Northway and was just about to unload there, when the CAA plane appeared, obviously trailing him. Reeve hurriedly fired up, took off ahead of them, keeping his log chain on their off-vision side. Back at Nabesna, Reeve jumped out of the cockpit, hustled to get the cowling, and replace it before his pursuers reappeared. When they landed, Reeve greeted the CAA men with a benign, innocent face—only to learn they were simply radio men from Washington who wanted nothing more than to see how operations were progressing at Northway!

—Beth Day, *Glacier Pilot: The Story of Bob Reeve and the Flyers Who Pushed Back Alaska's Air Frontiers*

$400 each to sit in the cramped fuselage of Model 40 mailplanes, just to get from Chicago to San Francisco in a hurry. These passengers represented the profit on Boeing's first mail route. How much more could the company make, William Boeing wondered, carrying a dozen travelers at a time?

The design and production process for the four original Model 80s was speedy even for the jazz age: they went from a gleam in Bill Boeing's bespectacled eye to the original sketch by chief engineer Charles N. "Monty" Montieth in late 1927, to the four practically finished airplanes shown in a panoramic photo of Plant One on the Duwamish River taken July 7, 1928.

The first Model 80 flew twenty days after the photo of the near-finished 80s was taken, and was delivered to BAT on August 8. The rush was so great that the plane had been in service for some months by the time its government Type Certificate—its license to fly, dated late October—caught up with it.

If the Model 80's overnight development seems unbelievable by today's standards, how about the unit price: $75,000! Altogether only sixteen were built: the four original ten-passenger Model 80s and eleven more improved, eighteen-passenger 80As. There was also a single luxury executive transport, the Model 226.

It was Edward Hubbard who got Boeing into the air transport business, eventually creating the need for the Model 80. Hubbard, who had been making money flying mail from Seattle to Victoria, British Columbia, wanted to bid for the contract to carry mail over Contract Air Mail (CAM) Route 18, from Chicago to San Francisco. Boeing's bid, based on Hubbard's income projections, careful calculations of expenses, and the planned performance of a new Boeing design, the Model 40A, was so low the Post Office Department demanded a personal half-million-dollar performance bond from Boeing himself. Winning CAM Route 18 got Boeing into the airliner business.

Hubbard's idea was to use the new 420-horsepower Pratt & Whitney Wasp air-cooled radial engine the company was installing in the F2B fighters it was producing for the

U.S. Navy. Hubbard pointed out that installing the Wasp in Boeing's Model 40, a mailplane that had lost a Post Office design competition a couple of years before, would produce a plane that not only met the Post Office's specifications but could carry two passengers as well. The nine-cylinder Wasp was itself lighter than the competition's ten-year-old Liberty engines, and it had the further advantage of dispensing with the weight of coolant, radiators, and plumbing.

CAM 18 made money from the first month. Since the margin of profit was the two passengers the Model 40A carried, Bill Boeing naturally wondered whether a bigger plane, designed specifically to carry people rather than mail, might not make a lot more.

The Museum of Flight's Model 80A is the second one built and the only restored example of its kind left in the world. Registered NC224M, it was delivered to BAT (which later became United Air Lines) on September 19, 1929, was upgraded to 80A-1 status with that model's triple-rudder empennage the following October, and was fitted with new wheels and brakes—brakes!—in August 1932.

The plane had three distinct careers. United Air Lines flew it until 1934 and then sold it, after five years in storage, to Monterey Peninsula Airways, who modified it for barnstorming with a twenty-four-seat interior and a yellow paint job. Alton Walker paid $6,000 for it.

The Museum of Flight's founding artifact, Bob Reeve's 80A, was hauled to the Anchorage city dump early in 1963.

After two seasons of quickie joyride flights over small cities throughout the western and northwestern states, NC224M was judged to be worn out. It probably was. The plane reportedly made sixty-three flights and carried 1,700 passengers in a single day. But being worn out made it an ideal candidate for heavy freight hauling in Alaska, a living museum of obsolete airplanes.

In 1941, months before Pearl Harbor, the Department of Defense realized that America's Arctic was undefended. The Civil Aeronautics Authority (now the Federal Aviation Administration) contracted with the giant Morrison-Knudsen Company (M-K) to build an airfield for the defense of Alaska at Northway, midway between Whitehorse, in Canada's Yukon, and Fairbanks. (In 1942 the Japanese bombed Dutch Harbor, in the Aleutian Islands, and occupied one of them, Attu.)

The closest road link to the airfield site ended at Nabesna, fifty miles away. Everything to be used in constructing the airfield had to be flown in from there. Robert Reeve, the famous Alaskan bush pilot, was hired by M-K to ferry construction supplies to Northway. Reeve bought NC224M to do the job.

Designed to carry a maximum payload of slightly more than 4,000 pounds, Reeve's Model 80A, dubbed "Yellow Peril" for its barnstorming paint job, once carried an iron boiler to Northway that weighed almost three times that much.

"After a few days I never took off with less than 7,000 pounds," Reeve acknowledged many years later. "I've brought that plane in with engine failure with as high as a hundred percent overload."

Impressed by the 80A—especially as compared with the more advanced Ford Tri-Motors he had flown in Chile, which performed badly with an engine out—Reeve bought another, newer Boeing 80A, NC229M, for M-K. The Museum of Flight's 80A is a composite of the two planes. This is how they came to be combined:

Gillam Airways, run by Harold "Thrill-'em, Chill-'em, No-kill-'em" Gillam, inherited the M-K contract in 1943 and assigned Merle K. "Mudhole" Smith to fly oil drums into Northway in the 80As. Smith called it "a bad job to fly. One engine always quit in cold weather."

Sometimes more than one. On March 21, 1943, on takeoff from Anchorage, Smith's right engine failed. He managed to land NC224M, but ground-looped because of the lack of power on one side. Then another engine failed, probably the one on the nose. Unable to control the plane, Smith plowed through a hangar containing the fleet of Woodley Airways, wiping it out. Yellow Peril's upper-left wing was broken and the center motor mount gave way, leaving the engine hanging at a forty-five-degree angle.

Yet again, NC224M's luck held. Its sister ship, being the newer airplane, would normally have succeeded it in supplying Northway. But NC229M didn't have the huge freight door Reeve had hacked out of NC224M's fuselage. NC229M was cannibalized for parts to keep the older airplane flying. Yellow Peril's third career lasted into 1945, when it was replaced by war-surplus DC-3s.

It stood in a field near the Anchorage airport for fifteen years, was hauled to the city dump, and then was granted a reprieve from the usual within-a-week burial when *Anchorage Times* head photographer Harriss Darby spotted it and informed friends in Seattle. Jack Leffler, a United Air Lines pilot and later a trustee of the Pacific Northwest Aviation Historical Foundation (PNAHF), bought the plane in 1963. The 80A restoration was the reason for the PNAHF's origination and therefore was a link in the founding by the PNAHF of the Museum of Flight.

The Air Force shipped the 80A from Anchorage's Elmendorf AFB in a C-124 Globemaster on February 25, 1964, whereupon the second Boeing 80A built became the object of a sixteen-year restoration project sponsored by the Boeing Management Association. The massive job was finished barely in time for United Air Lines' fiftieth-anniversary celebration of airline stewardess service. The restored 80A was accepted on behalf of the Museum of Flight by William Boeing Jr. on October 18, 1964.

BOEING MODEL 80A AIRLINER

Dimensions

Overall wingspan 80ft

Overall length 55ft

Height 15ft 2in

Engines

Three Pratt & Whitney Hornets, 525hp each at 1,900rpm

Weight

Empty (18 passengers) 10,417lbs

Loaded 17,500lbs

Performance

Maximum speed 138mph

Cruise 125mph

Range 460mi

Service ceiling 14,000ft

Aeronca C-2

For most manufacturers, getting into production in the fall of 1929 would have been disastrous timing. The first production Aeronca C-2 flew on October 20, eight days before the stock market crashed. This coincidence was, in Aeronca's case, a stroke of good fortune. In the words of Peter M. Bowers, who has owned a slightly larger C-3, "It was virtually a powered glider, and the corresponding low operating cost was its saving grace in a depressed market."

The Aeronautical Corporation of America, "A company as small as its name was big," was a well-capitalized outfit when it was formed in November 1928, with half a million dollars on hand, and very well connected, having Sen. Robert A. Taft, son of the former president, on its board. Aeronca, as the company was more widely known, lacked only a place to operate, something to sell, and someone to design and build it.

All these shortcomings were addressed within a few months when Jean Roché, senior aeronautical engineer for the U.S. Army Air Service, was invited to demonstrate the outcome of the backyard project he had been plugging away at, on and off, since the early 1920s. The demonstration took place at Wright Field in Dayton, Ohio, then the Army's aircraft test site.

The Roché light plane was a tiny puddle-jumper, so ugly it was irresistible. It looked like a rowboat with a laughably small propeller at the point of the bow. A single thin exhaust pipe hung down the prow from an engine with its two cylinders poking out the sides. Next came a pair of wheels that seemed far too large for the rest of the plane, seemingly stuck on the keel. The pilot sat in the boat, without even a windshield but shaded by the wing, looking at a

Above: Peter M. Bowers's Aeronca C-3. *Left*: Bowers in his Aeronca C-3 with Edo floats on Lake Union, Seattle, 1952. *Facing page*: Aerial refueling, Alameda, 1930. Forest M. "Iron Hat" Johnson picks up a can of gasoline in an early Aeronca C-2. Johnson always flew his C-2 wearing a derby.

Peter Bowers in his C-3: "The traffic on the highway was moving faster than I was!"

Th-th-that's all, folks: Instrument panel of a C-3. The choke knob was standard equipment.

Aeronca C-2 for rent: $4 an hour, unlimited free mileage.

grand total of four instruments. An overhead tripod from which wires radiated out over the wing somehow held everything together at the front. The tail surfaces looked far too big for the rest of the plane. The board of directors of the Aeronautical Corporation of America was enchanted.

A colleague of Roché's, John Dohse, who helped build this contraption and had once taken it all the way up to 20,000 feet, demonstrated its charms in the air while Roché explained its safety features to the Aeronca brass on the ground.

It had a steel-tube fuselage, still far from universal during the 1920s, and wooden wings. Roché and Dohse were concerned about the craft's tiny motorcycle-type engine, which they felt had not been sufficiently developed for reliability. They agreed that in the event of engine failure, Dohse would simply glide back to the field as if to intentionally show off the safety inherent in its excellent gliding characteristics.

As for the still-missing factory, that was taken care of by the stock market crash. The Metal Aircraft Company's factory at Lunken Airport, near Cincinnati, was building an impressive seven-passenger, all-metal, high-wing cabin monoplane called the Flamingo, but it was not selling well. The twentieth Flamingo sat through the summer unsold. With the Great Crash, the company went out of business and sold its assets to Aeronca for a fraction of their worth. Aeronca was now located in a virtually new, heated brick-and-glass factory at what was then America's largest airport. Meanwhile, Aeronca made arrangements to have the 107-cubic-inch, 26-horsepower jewel of an engine that had been specially designed for the Roché plane manufactured in Detroit.

Once Aeronca took over the Roché project, success was immediate. Aeronca sold ninety C-2s, at the remarkably low price of $1,495, by the end of 1930. By June 1931, the price was reduced to $1,245. Not only was it inexpensive to buy, it was downright miserly to operate.

Every aviation great in America seemed charmed by the homely but sweet-flying C-2. The flamboyant racing

Bob Cansdale mainstreets with the Museum of Flight's C-2.

pilot Roscoe Turner jokingly demonstrated how to compensate for the C-2's lack of brakes by reaching out with his gloved hand and grabbing the tire. The famous racing and test pilot Jimmy Doolittle called it "an excellent little airplane."

Stanley Huffman flew one of the first C-2s from Lunken to New York's Roosevelt Field, nonstop, in ten hours and ten minutes on April 9th, 1930. Even at the minuscule fuel consumption of two gallons per hour from the eight-gallon tank, refueling in the air from small drums was necessary. The story was widely publicized, but, as Paul Matt tells us, "some said it was just a *cheap* publicity stunt."

Seventy-four more C-2s were built in 1931, but by then the company had decided to go ever-so-slightly upmarket. Despite Roché's concerns about defeating the original concept, Aeronca's chief engineer, Roger Schlemmer, designed the enlarged C-3, adding 6 cubic inches, 3 pounds, and a neck-snapping 7 horsepower (for a total of 36) to the Morehouse engine. A plywood board became seating for two. The slightly wider fuselage actually improved the C-2's aerodynamics.

Roché, however, being the cautious designer of a safe personal airplane that he was, took his 220 shares of Aeronca stock but kept his secure Army job at Wright Field (which replaced McCook when it was closed in 1927). He became a consultant to the company. Dohse went to work for Boeing in Seattle. Aeronca continued to develop the light-plane formula through World War II.

The Museum of Flight's C-2, N30RC, was donated in 1986 by the late Bob Cansdale, an airline pilot who flew Boeing 247 and DC-3 airliners on Pacific Northwest routes and was a familiar presence at fly-ins around Seattle.

Marginal Proposition

I bought my C-3, a model that flies and handles just like the C-2, in 1951, which was absolutely the low point on the curve of prices for old airplanes before the antique boom got under way, for $200. Mind you, the wood prop on the Aeronca was broken, so I had to buy a new prop. I think it cost me twenty-five dollars. And that was that. I also had a Luscombe at the time.

When I bought the C-3 I was a "second-degree bachelor," living in a houseboat on Lake Union in Seattle. I had put the Aeronca on floats, and I tied it up to the houseboat. I had an airplane then, but no car. I'd come home from work at Boeing, fire up the Aeronca, fly over the lake, and watch my friends in the sailboat races from the best seat in the house. It was just plain fun flying, a real fun thing. Just pure sport.

Take a look at the panel—there isn't much on it. The required instrumentation was a tachometer, oil temperature and oil pressure indicator, plus a nonsensitive altimeter. The single-ignition engine had an on/off toggle switch and the automotive carburetor had a choke handle on the panel. The on/off lever for the 8-gallon gas tank stuck out through the big Aeronca nameplate on the center of the panel, and the throttle was just below it, still on the panel.

Each pilot had a set of rudder pedals on the C-3, but there was only one control stick. It was an interesting operation for the right-seat pilot. With his left hand on the stick that was centered ahead of the left-hand seat, he had to reach beyond his left side with his right hand to work the throttle in the middle of the panel. The rudder pedals were so close together in each set that the pilot practically banged his ankle bones together. When flying solo it was easier to fly with the left foot on the left-side pilot's left rudder pedal, and the right foot on the right-side pilot's right pedal.

To fly two in the Aeronca, you either had to really like the other person, because of the enforced togetherness, or sit at a slight angle so that the shoulders were staggered.

I was also a glider pilot at the time, and flying the Aeronca was much more like flying a glider than flying the Luscombe. If you did a lot of flying in C-3s, you could acquire a lot of bad habits by conventional power-plane standards. With only single ignition, one did not make a pre-takeoff mag check; if the engine was running the magneto was OK. Also, one did not apply carburetor heat when coming in to land; carb heat was permanently on. Similarly, one did not hold at the side of the runway for a full-throttle runup in a no-brakes airplane.

With its light weight and generous rudder area, the C-3 had even more trouble than its lightweight contemporaries (like the Taylor E-2 Cub) while taxiing downwind or in crosswinds. Sometimes the pilot could manage to get it pointed in the right direction, only to have the wind turn it back upwind like a weather vane.

Watching the weather-vane procedure at a modern small airport, the people on the line wonder what that nut thinks he's doing out there circling around like that. They either don't know or have forgotten that it used to be part of a line boy's job to run out into the field to grab a wingtip and steer a no-brakes light plane back to the line.

Taxiing downwind in a strong wind with no brakes and a tail skid that slides instead of digging in can be an exercise in sheer terror when there are obstacles ahead. It takes both savvy and willpower to realize and act on the fact that the only way to miss something you are obviously going to hit is to open the throttle, push the stick forward to raise the tail, and kick hard rudder to make a fast turn. With the C-3 and its kind, there is no other way.

The Aeronca engine sounded like no other, and the presence of only two cylinders had little to do with it. Where the old 90hp Curtiss OX-5 ran wide open at 1,400rpm (sometimes), the 1929 Kinner K-5 delivered its 100hp at 1,800rpm, and the little 90hp Velie-cum-Lambert radial turned 1,900, the Aeronca E-113A turned 2,400 wide open and cruised at 2,250 or more. Its sound was more like a continuous buzz than the pop-pop one would expect from two cylinders. Some people added twin ignition and magnetos, and that gave a little extra power, but that could snap the crankshaft. So you could have a bit too much of a good thing.

It's slow. You're going down to a fly-in at, say, Portland. You're batting along, just batting along—how else could you describe it?—you're heading down the main highway and the traffic on the highway is moving faster than you are!

I have checked other pilots out on my C-3, even when it was on floats, but I checked them out solo. It was such a marginal proposition getting off the water, you just wouldn't make it sometimes with two people aboard. So I'd show them around the cockpit—how much was there to learn?—and send them off.

With no airspeed indicator, it was fun to watch the guys take off. Not knowing how fast they were going, they would just go full speed ahead, get the tail up, and then when they took off they'd climb out real shallow, they didn't know how close they were to the stall speed. Same with landing. By carrying too much speed, they'd float and float and float the length of the runway and not get it down because they still didn't know the stall speed.

Finally, after more instruction from me, they'd end up flying the way it was meant to be flown, which is by feel. Finally, though, I installed an airspeed indicator. I don't know why, maybe the complaints got to me, but I put it up in the wing root so you'd have to turn around and make an effort to see it.

I had only two forced landings with it. Having the engine stop is not that much of a problem in the Aeronca: you can land it practically anywhere. On one of them, I just happened to be over Boeing Field, which is actually not the best place to do it. But the engine didn't just quit, it seized up. Now, a plane in distress is supposed to have the right-of-way, but at Boeing Field that might not make much difference. With no radio, you're in no position to argue. I just spiraled down, and suddenly there was this DC-6 on final approach. I wasn't going to get in front of him, so I just landed on the parallel taxiway instead.

No sooner had I come to a stop than this police car comes roaring up, lights flashing, siren wailing. The cop gets out and starts asking what the heck I'm doing here in this... thing. Just as he gets to me, his radio calls him. It's the tower. The voice on the radio says tell the guy in the light plane that he made a nice dead-stick landing.

—Peter M. Bowers, Aeronca C-3 owner

"This aircraft marks the emergence of general aviation in the United States," recalls Jay Spenser, of the Museum of Flight's curatorial staff, in his book *Aeronca C-2: The Story of the Flying Bathtub*. "Flying for the average American was not possible with the large and expensive airplanes of the day." The price could be as high as thirty dollars an hour in scarce early-Depression dollars. The Aeronca C-2 reduced that figure to about four dollars.

Although Aeronca light-plane production didn't last much past the war, its lovable little C-2 spawned a legion of competitors that eventually gave us the thousands of Pipers, Cessnas, and Beeches that now populate satellite airports throughout North America.

Bob Cansdale demonstrates the inherent stability and effortless ground handling of the Flying Bathtub. *Below*: Bob Cansdale in his Aeronca C-2, followed closely by Peter Bowers in his C-3.

43

DESIGNER: JEAN ROCHE

Jean Roché came to New York City from France in 1906, when he was twelve. He became a member of the New York Model Aero Club, making pocket money by carving small propellers from laminated wood. He regularly won prizes for the excellent flight characteristics of his models. Young Roché haunted the airfields of Long Island and learned to fly a hang-glider.

In 1911 he conceived an airfoil that would stabilize an aircraft in rough air. He applied for and received a patent, and renewed it three years later when he was twenty. It never sold.

After his graduation from Columbia in mechanical engineering, Roché was involved in the development of several airplanes. In 1917 he answered the U.S. Army's call for aeronautical engineers to help close the gap between American aviation and the fast-developing wartime state of the art in Europe. He was assigned to McCook Field, where he became part of an elite corps that included future Boeing chief engineer Charles N. "Monty" Montieth and I. M. "Mac" Laddon, who designed the Consolidated flying boats and B-24 Liberator bomber.

The immediate origins of the Roché light plane lay in a glider his superiors at McCook had asked him to design in 1923. Despite the handicap of being equipped with the upper wing panels from a Curtiss JN-4 biplane, the GL-2 glider flew well. Gen. Billy Mitchell liked it.

Roché was in a position to absorb the latest technology and apply it to his personal theories about stability in flight, which he considered the most desirable property of any flying machine. A new wing airfoil, the Clark Y, was being tested in the wind tunnel at Massachusetts Institute of Technology and seemed to offer the characteristics he had tried to design into his own patented airfoil nearly ten years before. He decided to use it on the maximum-safety airplane he had been thinking about.

He was having no such luck with an engine. He tried a German engine, but its maker took his deposit into bankruptcy. Roché and Dohse tried an 18hp Henderson motorcycle engine in 1924, but fortunately, considering its overheating tendencies, it was incapable of powering the Roché plane off the ground.

Once again, the answer practically fell into Roché's lap. Harold Morehouse, of the Wright Field powerplant section, was assigned to build a small engine for pumping

air into blimps. He was persuaded to enlarge his design to 80 cubic inches. The Morehouse engine was a success from the start, taking the Roché plane into the air during the intended taxi tests on the evening of September 1, 1925, and flying Dohse, who had little flight experience, on a five-mile circle of Wright Field. The engine never missed a beat during the more than 200 test flights Dohse made that year.

In a crash caused by Dohse's overloading the plane with another passenger and attempting a low-level, low-speed, too-steep bank, the engine was destroyed. But the design was developed by Wright engineers into a 107-cubic-inch, 26hp beauty that the Wright Aeronautical Corporation contracted to manufacture in 1926.

Roché had built a better mousetrap, but aside from the engine contract nobody was biting, so he gave up on his dream in 1927. That year Wright Aeronautical canceled the engine contract. As it happened, the difficulties were blessings in disguise. They forced Roché to wait until the economy was about to collapse completely. "If there was ever a time to build small and economical airplanes," Jay Spenser observes, "this seemed to be it."

AERONCA C-2

Dimensions

Overall wingspan 36ft

Overall length 20ft

Height 7ft 6in

Weight

Empty 406lbs

Loaded 700lbs

Performance

Maximum speed 80mph

Cruise 65mph

Stall 31mph

Range 240mi

Service ceiling 16,500ft

Stearman PT-13A Kaydet and C-3B

How a nation teaches the arts of war can tell us more about its people than how it fights. More than other military aircraft of World War II, the trainers used in that conflict reflected the national temperaments of the combatants.

The Bucker Jungmeister, for example, was a precision aerobatic instrument, typically German in its functional beauty and careful detailing. The de Havilland Tiger Moth was frail and rudimentary; as with the British school system, to survive the Tiger Moth was to be prepared for anything.

But none of these was as much a product of national values as the American Stearman "Kaydet" trainer. Big, tough, durable, easy to fly but requiring constant attention to the controls, the Stearman trainer was—still is—an honest airplane. It was built in greater quantities than any other American biplane. Nearly half the 8,584 Stearman trainers built are still around, many of them kept airworthy by the equivalent of 1,762 more Stearmans available in spare parts.

Budd Davisson, who has flown many Stearmans, characterizes the rugged trainer not in female terms, as most pilots refer to airplanes, but rather as "a gentleman." "If you feel an overwhelming urge to crash an airplane, this is obviously the one to do it in, since the Kaydet will poke a hole in anything you decide to hit."

The trainer is one of two Stearman biplanes in the Museum of Flight. Both carry the Stearman trademark: handsome, strong, well-proportioned outlines. But only the C-3B mailplane is a true Stearman. The one airplane buffs would call "the Stearman"—the wartime Model 75 trainer, or PT-13A Kaydet as represented in the Museum of Flight's collection—is actually a Boeing product.

True Stearmans, such as the 1931 C-3B, were products of one of the most distinguished lines of aircraft development during aviation's between-wars golden age. Stearman's motto was Dedicated to the Discriminating Buyer, and the discriminating buyer would have known that the Stearmans were developed by an all-star team of engineers.

Stearman C-3B mailplane. *Facing page*: The U.S. Army Air Corps takes delivery of the 1,000th Kaydet.

Lloyd Carlton Stearman's designs flew right because they looked right. They looked right partly because he was not an aircraft engineer but an architect-in-training whose studies were interrupted by World War I. He served in naval aviation during the war, finished his studies in architecture, and was working for an architect in Wichita when E. M. "Matty" Laird arrived to help make that prairie city the "Aviation Capital of the World."

Matty Laird was brought to Wichita from Chicago by wealthy oilman Jake Moellendick to start an airplane factory in 1919. (Laird, nearly forgotten today, was later the designer of planes that won the Thompson Trophy three times and the transcontinental Bendix Trophy once.) Joining him were three future presidents of aircraft manufacturing companies: Buck Weaver, who founded the Waco (Weaver Aircraft Company) firm; Walter Beech of Beechcraft; and Stearman. Like most all-star teams, they didn't stay together long. Each had his own ideas about how to build airplanes.

Weaver and Laird left the Laird Airplane Company by 1922, but Beech and Stearman stayed on for three more years. In 1923 Laird sold the business to his employees, who named the company Swallow Aircraft Company. Stearman is credited with designing the lovely "New Swallow" mailplane in 1924, a 1926 example of which survives in the collection of the Museum of Flight.

But Beech and Stearman disagreed with Moellendick's policy of building with stick-and-wire techniques and left together, teaming up with Clyde Cessna to found the legendary Travel Air Manufacturing Company in early 1925.

Stearman went to California in 1926 after barely a year with Travel Air. At Clover Field in Santa Monica, in early 1927, he and his longtime assistant Mac Short introduced the first C-1 Sport Commercial biplanes, built with Curtiss OX-5 or Hispano-Suiza engines at his Venice plant. He returned to Wichita later that year and mated his C-3 airframes with 220-horsepower Wright J-5 Whirlwind radial engines similar to the one that powered Charles Lindbergh's Ryan NYP across the Atlantic.

This combination, the C-3B, was only slightly different from any other radial-engined biplane, but there was something about these ships—the streamlined spinner, perhaps,

U.S. ARMY PT-17
AIR CORPS SERIAL NO.
CREW WEIGHT 400 LBS

1000

FIRE EXTING

or the big wheels hanging from split-axle landing gear—that looked to be worth every nickel of their $8,970 price. The C-3B was awarded its type certificate in July 1928. The Museum of Flight's example, built in 1931, is marked to represent one of five operated by Western Air Express on its Cheyenne-Denver-Pueblo airmail route beginning December 10, 1927. It was found derelict in Nevada in 1963 and restored over six years by R. J. McWhorter of Prosser, Washington.

The Stearman Aircraft Company joined William E. Boeing's giant United Aircraft & Transport Corporation in 1929. But Stearman could abide working for someone else only until 1931, when he left again for California and formed a partnership with Walter Varney, an early customer for Stearman's C-3s. By 1939, Stearman Aircraft had become the Wichita Division of Boeing.

If life in the aviation world of Wichita had seemed like a game of musical chairs, it was the same in California. In 1932, just thirty-four years of age, Stearman was president of the reorganized Lockheed Aircraft Corporation of Burbank, a job that held his attention for a full three years. His next career move was unfortunate. He left Lockheed to spend two years marketing a prize-winning but now forgotten safety plane. This was just before the best-known product of his onetime company, the airplane known by the generic title "Stearman," became a mass-produced, profitable wartime item.

That was the Stearman Kaydet series of military training aircraft. Although Lloyd Stearman was long gone from the company by the time it appeared, the Stearman Model 70, as the first one was designated, reflected the same philosophy of building with heavy-gauge metal tubing

Stearman PT-17 Kaydet basic trainer. *Facing page*: Neither snow, nor rain, nor heat, nor gloom of night: The U.S. Post Office pioneered night flying with such aircraft as the Stearman C-3B.

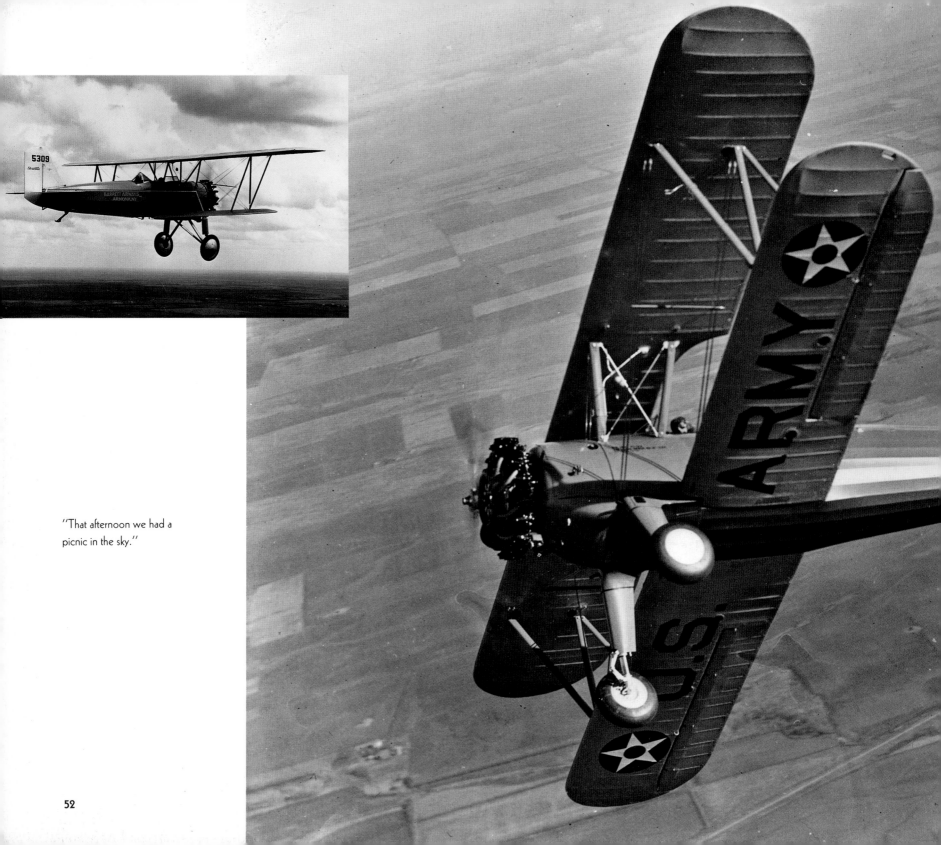

"That afternoon we had a
picnic in the sky."

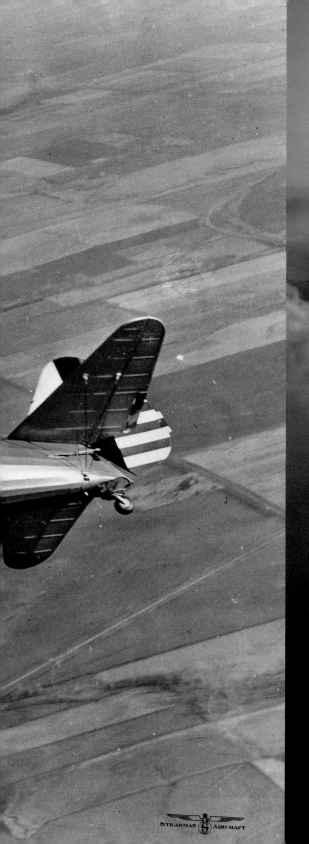

The Earth Above, the Sky Below

Robert S. Johnson, a World War II twenty-eight-victory ace over Europe, felt fortunate to have trained on Stearmans with H. E. Fulk, "mild-mannered and a fabulous flier." This passage describes the moment when Johnson convinces Fulk he has the makings of a combat pilot:

... I had just completed a chandelle with the Stearman when Fulk came on the speaking tube: "Cadet Johnson, I've got it." I released the controls and looked forward in the small mirror. For a moment I could have sworn the quiet, soft-spoken instructor had a gleam in his eye; knowing Fulk, however, I dismissed the thou—

WHAM! Earth horizon and sky and clouds and Stearman engine whipped crazily around in a whirling streak. The trainer's nose snapped up and around, a stomach-wrenching whip combined with a rapid rolling motion.

"What was that?" I shouted.

Fulk laughed. "A snap roll, Johnson. How did you like it?"

"I don't know what to ... I love it, Sir! ..."

He chuckled. "Hang on," he called. "Here we go again. A bit more gentle this time; I'll slow roll her through."

The wings tilted to the left as Fulk swung the Stearman into a turn. But ... as we reached a bank of forty-five degrees from the horizontal I felt Fulk's foot holding opposite rudder. Instead of turning, the Stearman continued to roll; the wings kept swinging around until, for a split second, they stood vertically along the horizon. Then we were going over, rolling smoothly into inverted flight.

I didn't know what to expect, but I followed Fulk through on the controls to feel the reactions of the ship in the slow roll. Then we were inverted—and I never expected the stream of dirt, nuts, paper and other debris that dropped from the cockpit floor and fell past my face. For a moment my sight was obscured by the flow of debris that swirled about my face before the propeller blast whipped it away.

Before I had time even to think about the dirt flying past, I dropped suddenly. The belt tugged against my stomach as I hung suspended. Unhappily I realized one disadvantage of being a sandblower—my feet fell away from the controls. There I was, hanging upside down, my feet unable to reach the controls. A fine picture of a pilot I was then!

I waved my left hand about frantically, trying to grab something to give me support. Still inverted, I found a metal tube along the side of the seat and hung on tightly.

I had sense enough to look about. My first sight of a world flung upside down was fabulous. Looking straight "up" I saw trees black against the snow, and "below" me stretched the deep blue sky. The wind streamed past my helmet and goggles, and, strangely, the roar of the engine had become a pleasant and muted sound. And then we were coming out, rolling around again until the earth rested below and the sky stretched away above me.

The first thing I did was to reach down and tighten my safety belt as far as it would go.

"Johnson, do you want to do one? ..."

... That afternoon we had a picnic in the sky. Fulk was feeling his oats, and he slow rolled, barrel rolled, and snap rolled, easing the Stearman through her maneuvers as if he were part of the biplane's nervous system....

—Robert S. Johnson with Martin Caidin, *Thunderbolt!*

that he had advocated since 1926. It was Harold Zipp and Jack Clark who designed the Model 70 for Boeing in 1933. The prototype was quickly put together late that year, and it was test-flown before the year was out.

A dozen years in production for a design that took months from the drawing board to the air is a singular example of industrial economy. So were the planes themselves: their costs to the government declined from a high of $10,412 for the PT-13A down to $7,713 for the PT-27. The Navy ordered the first of its NS-1s (Model 73) in 1934, and the Air Corps bought PT-13s (Model 75) in 1936. With wartime radial engines that put out 220hp, the big, sturdy airframe would correct most mistakes a novice pilot could possibly make.

"Naturally," Budd Davisson points out, "the 450-horse R-985 (Pratt & Whitney Wasp Jr.) conversions change that story quite a bit, and 600-horse airshow machines and sprayers are a different tune altogether. Those with the R-1340 Wasp up front seem to hunker down at the end of a runway and leap straight up...."

Most Stearman Kaydets that survived into peacetime became crop dusters, and a handful of heavily modified ones are still in action. The Museum of Flight's Kaydet was built by Boeing Wichita in 1937 as the fifty-fifth PT-13A off the line. It was converted to a PT-13C by being fitted with a more powerful 280hp Lycoming radial. It was converted to civilian status after 1945 and retired in 1950, "destroyed beyond repair." The wreck was bought in 1962 by a Seattle businessman, Francis Londo, who did a comprehensive restoration, returning the Stearman to PT-13A specs (except for powering it with a 220hp Continental radial). William I. Phillips of Bellevue, Washington, who bought it in 1977, donated it in airworthy condition to the Museum in 1983.

In the Great Gallery of the Museum of Flight, the C-3B shows off its Wright J-5 "Whirlwind" engine, considered the first truly reliable aircraft powerplant after Lindbergh used one to cross the Atlantic. *Facing page*: More than 10,000 Kaydet trainers were produced under various model names and designations between 1936 and 1945. Three thousand were still on the FAA civil register 25 years after World War II.

STEARMAN MODEL 75, PT-13A

Dimensions

Overall wingspan 32ft 2in

Overall length . . . . 24ft ¼in

Height 9ft 2in

Engine

Various. Most PT-13As had one Lycoming 9-cylinder, air-cooled radial engine, 220hp.

Weight

Empty 1,936lbs

Loaded 2,717lbs

Performance

Maximum speed 124mph

Cruise 106mph

Range (at cruise, 65% power) 505mi

Boeing 247D

The Boeing 247 was the smooth new shape of aviation in 1933, formed in streamlined metal and glass: a commercial transport that was faster than most military airplanes then in service. So clearly did it show the way that it was quickly superseded by the rush of new designs it inspired. After its year of lighting up the sky as the first "three-mile-a-minute" airliner—the plane that cut seven hours off the San Francisco–New York time—the 247 began to fade from the scene, relegated to secondary routes by the advent of the Douglas DC series.

While the 247 was briefly the most advanced transport in the world, the transitional nature of its design was evident in certain backward-looking features that were changed on the updated 247D. The most obvious of these was its forward-sloping windshield. More important, the plane's thick wing, designed for maximum lift, ran its spars through the passenger cabin, creating an awkward leather-covered barrier for passengers to step over. And there were no wing flaps. This mixed personality reflected arguments within the Boeing Company's engineering staff over how far the 247 design should push the state of the art.

But the 247's main handicap was its conservative carrying capacity. It had room for ten passengers; the later DC-3 carried twenty-one. Furthermore, airplane technology was changing so rapidly during the mid-thirties that new-model engines could render planes without them instantly obsolete. The 247's Pratt & Whitney engines developed 550 horsepower, while the DC-1's Wright Cyclones offered 710hp for takeoff.

Seen as an early product of Boeing's long-term determination to crack the airliner market, the 247 was only a mixed, brief success. Nevertheless, the plane took the Boeing Airplane Company to the technological forefront of the aviation industry worldwide, a position it has retained ever since.

What suddenly changed the company from a builder of fabric-skinned biplanes to the world-beating designer of revolutionary all-metal transports and bombers?

Harold Mansfield, author of *Vision*, credits Edward Hubbard with urging Boeing to build all-metal airplanes in

The Boeing 247 made history as the first all-metal, twin-engine monoplane airliner with retractable landing gear. *Below*: The prototype of the first three-mile-a-minute airliner on an early test flight, 1933. The 247 could carry 10 passengers coast to coast in only 20 hours.

Model 247s being built at Boeing's Plant 1, February 1933. *Below:* United Air Lines 247D loading at Boeing Field.

1928. Hubbard had considerable influence with company vice president Clairmont Egtvedt: he had operated one of the first profitable airmail routes, Seattle to Victoria, British Columbia, and it had been his idea to mate an existing biplane design with the Pratt & Whitney Hornet engine to create the Model 40A, which made money from the start on Boeing's Contract Air Mail Route 18, Chicago to San Francisco.

Since the 95 had a metal-lined baggage compartment so the airmail bag locks wouldn't tear the fabric, and metal access plates for the powerplant, it seemed natural to Hubbard that Boeing's next transport should be built entirely of metal, "nose to tail."

Egtvedt picked up a piece of paper, sketched a round fuselage—the easiest shape to render in metal—and placed it on top of a monoplane wing. Simple. But there was no landing gear, Hubbard noted in wonderment. Egtvedt, Boeing's

former chief engineer, thought the drag caused by fixed gear cost more per mile than the payload. So he proposed that the landing gear retract into the wings. That, in a nutshell, is Mansfield's account of the origin of the Model 200 Monomail, the first Boeing design to have a proper name and the first truly modern Boeing airplane.

Besides listening carefully, Egtvedt had another way of moving the company ahead: he made sure young talent was served. The Boeing VP had himself become chief engineer very soon after joining the company straight out of school, and was running the company after less than ten years. There was no shortage of eager young minds around Boeing by 1930. The rotund Bob Minshall became design engineer on the Monomail because of his quick creativity, while Lysle Wood designed the monocoque fuselage. Both would be deeply involved in the design of the 247.

Boeing's chief engineer at the time, Charles N. "Monty" Montieth, was not so sure an airplane such as the one sketched by Egtvedt would be safe. In his time as an Army Air Corps procurement officer at Wright Field, in Ohio, Montieth had seen one colleague killed and another barely escape a midair breakup, both of them in monoplanes. His worry was that making planes faster would impose stresses on them that were not yet fully understood.

Other companies had been building monoplanes for some time. Lockheed had taken the lead in single-wing development with its Vega, a high-wing design built from molded plywood, designed by the young John K. Northrop. Northrop was the most forward-thinking airplane engineer in America. He moonlighted from designing the Lockheed Vega to do detail improvements to the Ryan M-2 monoplane, adding speed and extending its range to make possible Charles Lindbergh's New York–to–Paris solo flight of May 21, 1927.

The Vega flew July 4 of that year and went on to establish thirty-four world records for speed and endurance in the hands of such pilots as Wiley Post and Amelia Earhart. Lockheed, more than satisfied with the best-selling private aircraft in the world from 1927 to 1932, refused to move ahead to the all-metal designs Northrop wanted to build.

Northrop, a "tireless uphill swimmer," in the words of his biographer and business associate Ted Coleman, founded his own company in mid-1928 to build the most advanced aircraft in the world. The new firm, Avion, began operations in 1929. This was not the most opportune time to start a new business venture. In quick succession, Northrop produced two all-metal aircraft, the Alpha seven-passenger transport and the prototype two-seat racing Beta.

Sales of airplanes of all types were declining in 1930. William E. Boeing, a longtime admirer of Northrop, heard of Avion's cash-flow problems, flew to California to assess the company, and persuaded his holding company, United Aircraft & Transport Corporation, to buy Northrop out. The deal was closed in 1931.

So Boeing was thinking about all-metal construction as early as 1928— the year it built the fabric-covered Model 80 trimotor airliners—and then acquired the most advanced all-metal techniques in America in 1931. Only two Monomails were built because engine and propeller technologies were not sufficiently developed to take full advantage of the design's potential. The Monomail first flew in May 1930 and led Egtvedt to wonder about the load-carrying possibilities of a twin-engined, all-metal monoplane. Minshall went to work on an entry in the U.S. Army Air Corps' 1931 bomber competition that promised a quantum advance in military airplane technology.

The Boeing B-9 bomber, which first flew in April 1931, was faster than contemporary fighters, even though it retained such drag-creating features as open cockpits and gun positions, and carried its bombload under its wings. The prototype lost the competition and subsequent production contract when Glenn Martin's engineers made an eleventh-hour, three-week effort to improve their entry, mainly by bringing the crew and bombs indoors. Only seven YB-9s were built.

It took courage to go ahead with as advanced an airliner design as the 247 after so few of its predecessors had been built, at a time when most airlines were still operating biplanes and when Boeing's chief engineer, Montieth, had his doubts about the new design's safety. This was especially true considering that when Boeing had canvassed the airlines in its system for their ideas on a new airliner, the response had been anything but a consensus.

Boeing proceeded with at least three design studies for a new transport during the early 1930s. Each was a direct response to a particular airline's preferences.

The Model 238 was a fifteen-passenger, shoulder-winged monoplane trimotor with fixed landing gear. Next came the 239, a biplane trimotor with fixed but streamlined, spatted gear. National Air Transport liked the biplane configuration, but the middle engine in the nose made for a noisy cockpit and bad forward visibility.

Boeing often used its own employees for its promotional pictures. Right front: A pensive Ed Wells, designer of the 247's tail surfaces. All are eating Washington apples.

The 247's generous wing
area made for docile han-
dling, "like a smaller B-17,"
says Harold "Kit" Carson.

Best in Show

The Museum of Flight's Boeing 247 was acquired in more or less flyable condition and appeared at air shows throughout the American West during its years as the star attraction of the Museum's founding organization, the Pacific Northwest Aviation Historical Foundation. The plane's most frequent pilots were Jack Leffler, the United Air Lines captain who found it, and Harold "Kit" Carson, a wartime flying instructor on Boeing B-17 and B-29 bombers and a postwar production test pilot, flight safety officer, and corporate pilot for the Boeing Company. Carson had flown 247s during a two-year hiatus from Boeing in the early 1950s.

Both pilots enjoyed flying this 247—especially because, with its interior stripped for spraying, the tank removed, and more powerful 600hp Pratt & Whitney engines installed for overweight operations, the plane is a bit of a hot rod.

Before they flew it from Bakersfield, Leffler and Ray Pepka had mechanics look the 247 over, but could find no pilot willing to check Leffler out on it. Its landing gear had not been cycled in six years, so Leffler left the wheels down. Otherwise the aircraft seemed flyable, so they flew the thousand miles to Seattle, stopping at Fresno, Red Bluff, Medford, Portland, and Auburn, with Leffler improvising as they went.

Leffler: *I'm not a daredevil. I've seen the elephants and heard the owls. We were careful. It was a very light airplane; I walked the throttles, and before I got to full power on the manifold gauge, we were flying. I never did make a bad landing in it, not even the first one.*

When I got back [from Bakersfield], I told someone, maybe Bill Allen [then president of Boeing], "I wish someone would build them again." The tail is very light with the seats out. United pilots used to taxi them with the tail in the air. Mind you, you have to play the brakes pretty easy; you could nose it over doing that. Believe me, there are tapes showing them doing it; you'd taxi up to the terminal and gently let the tail down.

Carson: *My reaction to this plane was that it was a very docile airplane, quite forgiving. It flies like a smaller B-17. Its takeoff and landing characteristics were very similar. It was an easy airplane to land: approach at sixty to seventy knots, and at that speed you were in the right attitude for a three-point landing. A slight flare and you were on the ground. Get the tail up and it would fly itself right off the ground. A docile airplane, and it cruised, too; you just got up there and sat down and it did the work.*

Leffler: *It's heavy on the controls. There is no boost. It's a manual-control airplane; it's not like the DC-3, Lord no. You put an aileron down, and you wait for the response. You kick it to see if it's alive.*

Carson: *Most of the time we flew it, the 247 had no radio. We had this portable radio and we stuck the antenna out the window to talk to the tower.*

We went to an air show at Shelton one Sunday. Shelton was socked in, but the fixed-base operator thought it would be opened up by the time we got there. So we took off from Boeing Field, where it was totally VFR [Visual Flight Rules, the pilot's term for clear weather]. Three minutes after we took off Seattle-Tacoma was closed

down. We decided to head for McChord Field. By the time we got there, it was closed down. We thought, "OK, let's try for Shelton." We got there and we could see it was clouded over, but there was a hole in the clouds, and we could see the end of the runway through the hole. The operator said he had no activity. So down we went. It so happened that we came down right in front of the grandstand. People were filing into the seats, but of course, with the weather, they hadn't expected to see much. We came in at seventy-five–eighty knots, right by the stands. We got Best in Show. People were always impressed by the airplane.

Leffler: *Of course the 247 didn't have any flaps. We were taking it down to L.A. [during the Western Airlines anniversary tour] and we were starting our descent into L.A. when we lost oil pressure in one engine. Spanky Allen was with me as copilot and engineer. Even with one engine throttled back and compensating with the rudder, we used only half the strip. An old-timer came up to me and complimented me on the landing: "Jack, you didn't even use your flaps." I said, "Didn't they come down?"*

Carson: *I've often compared the 247s ... if that plane had had the technical instrumentation, radio capability, navigation instruments, it would have been comparable to the 727. The plane had a questionable history; a few of them were lost in bad weather. Boy, a modern navigation system, it would be a great airplane.*

Leffler: *I got my reward from watching so many people just come up and fondle and touch it.*

—From interviews, November 1989

The third scheme, the Model 243, incorporated two of the more powerful Hornet engines Pratt & Whitney was developing. This was progress, but the plane still had the high wing, whose long struts effectively precluded retractable landing gear. Boeing Air Transport saw the advantages of a twin, although the other airlines felt that the reliability of P&W's proven 550hp Wasp would make three of them preferable to two of the newer, more powerful Hornets. Their concern centered on the possible effects of loss of an engine on one of their Rocky Mountain routes.

In the face of these preferences, it is impressive that the company put its doubts aside and went ahead with a low-wing monoplane twin. On September 2, 1931, work order number 9045 authorized 250 work-hours for preliminary design on what was designated the Model 247.

By that winter the 247 looked good enough on paper that preliminary drawings and performance estimates were used to sell the newly formed United Air Lines on the idea of replacing its entire fleet with sixty 247s.

Boeing had never received an order for anything like that many civil aircraft, let alone right off the drawing board. Paradoxically, that success would sow the seeds for the 247's speedy demise, leaving Boeing unable to supply any other airlines with the pace-setting 180-mile-per-hour airliner for more than a year. United's competition would go to Douglas Aircraft for something even better.

Detail design began in February 1932. Almost a year later the first 247 took to the air, on February 8, 1933. At the end of March the first production machine was handed over to Boeing Air Transport.

With all-metal construction and low-wing configuration; trim tabs to lessen the effort of moving its control surfaces; retractable landing gear to minimize drag; the proven supercharged Wasp powerplants; and variable-pitch, three-bladed propellers that could be set to a fine angle for takeoff and coarse pitch for economical cruising, the 247 incorporated features that had never been combined on a single airplane. It also introduced air-conditioned cabins to the commercial airways.

The Museum of Flight's Boeing 247, factory number 1729 and the forty-seventh of the seventy-five built, pro-vides an example of how useful the plane could be even long after it had been superseded on main-line routes. One of four 247s left in the world, it has been owned by eleven organizations and has carried the insignia of several more since it was delivered to Pacific Air Transport, a division of Boeing Air Transport, on July 26, 1933. Pacific Air Transport became part of United Air Lines on May 1, 1934, and new insignia were applied. It was upgraded to 247D specifications in 1935, with new engine cowlings, propellers, and control surfaces, but retained its forward-sloping windshield, a reminder that it is one of the original 247s. Two years later it was sold to Pennsylvania-Central Airlines.

Number 1729 spent most of World War II in Canada, carrying civil markings as a government transport, Royal Canadian Air Force roundels and serial number 7839 as one of eight that flew with the RCAF, and then airline insignia again with Maritime Central Airways. By the end of 1945 it was back in the United States with Columbia Airlines, having logged 16,211 hours in the air. After a nose-over on landing in Puerto Rico in 1952, it was not flown for two years. Converted to a crop sprayer in 1955, it passed through the hands of four owners in little more than a year.

Jack Leffler, a Museum of Flight founder who flew United Air Lines equipment from the DC-3 to the 747 over thirty-six years, spotted the 247 parked off the ramp at Bakersfield, California. Ray Pepka, a former trustee of the Museum and a Boeing subcontractor, put up the money to buy it for the Pacific Northwest Aviation Historical Foundation (PNAHF) in 1966.

Its original registration number, NC13347, was reapplied by the PNAHF, founders of the Museum of Flight. Cosmetically restored, the 247 wore 1930s United Air Lines livery, but it was repainted in the colors of Western Air Express in 1976 to celebrate Western Airlines' fiftieth anniversary. In mid-September 1979 the 247 was committed to a full, ground-up rebuild. By 1988, George Juneau, a Boeing retiree and the 247 restoration crew chief, working two shifts a day at the Museum of Flight's Paine Field facility, had put 10,000 hours of his time—the equivalent of 250 working weeks—into the plane as a tribute to its historic status as one of the first modern airliners.

BOEING 247

Dimensions

Overall wingspan	74ft
Overall length	51ft 4in
Height	15ft 5in

Engines (247D)

Two Pratt & Whitney Wasps,
550hp at 2,200rpm at 8,000ft

Weight

Empty	8,400lbs
Loaded	12,650lbs

Performance

Maximum speed (247D)	200mph
Cruise	189mph
Range (273gal)	745mi
Payload	10 passengers, baggage, 400lbs mail
Absolute ceiling	27,200ft

Douglas DC-3

Before 1931, Transcontinental & Western Airlines (TWA), "The Lindbergh Line," with the transatlantic Lone Eagle as a major stockholder, symbolized safety in the air. Then, on March 31, 1931, a trimotor TWA Fokker F.10 crashed in a wheat field near Bazar, Kansas, killing eight people, including Knute Rockne, the famous Notre Dame football coach. The Fokker's wooden wing had broken up in a thunderstorm.

Wooden wings were soon outlawed on American commercial transports, and TWA (later Trans World Airlines) quickly replaced its fleet with all-metal Ford Tri-Motors. The "Tin Goose" was only a little more than half as fast as the 180-mile-per-hour Boeing 247s United Air Lines had already ordered straight off the drawing boards. TWA realized that the sixty 247s United was to acquire in 1933 would render every other airline's equipment instantly obsolete.

Jack Fry, TWA's twenty-nine-year-old boy wonder vice president, sent a letter dated August 2, 1932, to several aircraft manufacturers announcing that his airline would buy ten or more all-metal, twelve-passenger trimotor airliners. Donald Douglas has called this letter "the birth certificate of the modern airliner."

Douglas Aircraft, too, was aware of the Boeing 247. Before Boeing's revolutionary transport flew, a huge sign in the Douglas Aircraft Company plant at Santa Monica displayed a cutaway of the 247 with the caption Don't Copy It! Do It Better!

Only ten days after receiving the letter and its accompanying specifications, two Douglas Aircraft Company engineers left Burbank, California, for New York with the company's proposal. By using the new radial engines being developed by Wright and Pratt & Whitney—as Boeing had on its 247—Douglas thought it could offer a twin with better performance than the current trimotors.

This design, the DC-1, instantly surpassed the 247 in speed, comfort, and payload. When TWA ordered it, Douglas stock more than doubled in value, to sixteen dollars. But to develop the one and only DC-1, Douglas Aircraft spent almost twice the $125,000 advance TWA had paid—in gold—on its order for a new airliner. The DC-1 flew July 1, 1933. (Boeing's 247 had flown for the first time that March.) This was a historic moment: it marked the beginning of American supremacy in commercial aviation.

After designing and building a series of mostly military biplanes, including the Douglas World Cruisers that were the first aircraft to fly around the world in 1924, Donald Douglas had made way for brighter, younger engineers. In 1933

Facing page: United Air Lines DC-3 *City of Seattle. Above:* United Air Lines had the first modern airliners in 1934 with the Boeing 247, left. Within months the 247 had been eclipsed by the Douglas DC-3. *Below:* The best customer for DC-3s was the U.S. Army Air Force, which bought some 10,000 under the designations C-47, C-53, and C-117. The C-47 was used in every combat area of World War II. Pictured here in Calcutta.

Douglas Aircraft was, perhaps more than at any other time, an engineering talent hothouse, with John K. Northrop, available because his company had been bought by William Boeing's United Aircraft and Transport conglomerate; chief engineer James H. "Dutch" Kindelberger, future head of North American Aviation, who had pushed for two engines instead of three on the DC-1; and Arthur Raymond, who figured out how to build Northrop's revolutionary multicellular wing for the DC-1 and would head the later DC-3 project.

Only one DC-1 was built because it was obvious how it could be improved. On its first flight, it was saved only by the skill of test pilot Carl Cover and engineer Fred Herman in the right-hand seat when the engines failed each time the aircraft assumed its climbing attitude. The problem was minor: the carburetor floats stopped the supply of fuel each time the aircraft's nose lifted. Over three days in May 1935 it set or broke twenty-two records, including eight world records.

By 1934 Douglas was still $266,000 behind after taking in $1,625,000 on TWA's launch order for twenty-five stretched DC-2s that sat two extra passengers in a longer cabin. It didn't hurt that a DC-2 won the transport division of the London-to-Melbourne MacRobertson Air Race. The KLM Royal Dutch Airlines DC-2 beat a 247 and finished second overall to the De Havilland Comet racer, built specially for the race. A nice touch was that KLM flew three passengers and a load of mail over the race route as it would have flown the same trip on a scheduled basis, with a

Two DC-3s at Boeing Field, Seattle, 1940, park outside the terminal according to passenger-door location. Left: a United Air Lines DST-A sleeper, with small upper-berth windows. Right: Northwest Airlines DC-3A.

regular crew. After fifty were built the DC-2 broke even. In fact, Douglas Aircraft was straining to keep up with orders for 200.

The last thing Donald Douglas figured he needed at that point was the order from American Airlines for twenty greatly modified "sleeper" versions with wider cabins. American was successfully operating biplane Curtiss Condor sleepers and was wedded to the concept of overnight air travel. C. R. Smith, American's president, kept after Douglas, offering to buy the twenty planes sight unseen. The company, uninspired, called the special project for American Airlines the Douglas Sleeper Transport (DST).

"So they buy twenty of our ships," Donald Douglas is reported to have complained. "We'll be lucky if we break even." Things only got worse as the bigger DST went through eleven wind-tunnel models and ate up $500,000 of the DC-2 profits.

The DC-2 won Donald Douglas the 1936 Collier Trophy. But the DC-2, as good as it was, still offered much room for improvement, as if the ideal airplane had been coming more and more into focus all the time. It needed only to be bigger. The DST project was started with an objective of making it as similar as possible to the DC-2: eighty-five percent parts commonality was the objective. But so extensively redesigned was the DST that only ten percent of its parts were from the DC-2. The DST added fifty percent to the DC-2's payload and, configured with seats instead of beds, added eight passengers to the DC-2's maximum of fourteen.

This was essentially the DC-3. It flew December 17, 1935. The first DST, with fourteen sleeper berths, was delivered to American Airlines in June 1936, followed in August by the first true DC-3, with twenty-one seats.

The DC-1–DC-3 series made Douglas the world leader in commercial transports. Long after the last DC-3 (and its military version, the C-47) had left the assembly line in 1946, Douglas was still first in the world as an airliner builder with the four-engine DC-4–DC-7 series, losing that status only at the dawn of the jetliner era when the Boeing 707 beat the DC-8 into the air. Douglas sold 609 DC-3s to the airlines and 10,046 C-47s to the armed forces of several countries during World War II. Ninety percent of the world's airline business was being flown in DC-3s by the time the war broke out. Douglas grossed an estimated one billion dollars on the DC-3.

Only in 1988 were the Canadian Armed Forces' last nine operational C-47s retired, mainly for lack of spare parts. It became lore that these Dakotas, as the British named them during the war, had grown a foot longer from being pulled through the air for so long. The surfaces of their wings were finely rippled from forty-five years of alternating tension and compression on the aluminum skins, which sculpted patterns into the alloy. They showed as clearly as X-rays the strong multicellular interior wing structure that Jack Northrop had developed during the early 1930s, making possible the most advanced aircraft of the time.

Northrop's great contribution to aircraft design was to change the wing from a set of assembled spars and ribs, covered with fabric, to a thick metal skin that carried much of the load itself, supported internally by a nearly indestructible network of welded boxes. Even if several members cracked or broke, the structure would hold.

Donald Douglas's personal tribute to Northrop, who headed the Douglas El Segundo Division from 1933 to 1937, was to say that every airplane built since then "has a little Northrop in it." Everything else about the DC-3, from its wind-tunnel–shaped aerodynamics to the passenger capacity that guaranteed its commercial success, flowed from the load-carrying capacity of its wing.

This wing had a couple of additional advantages. It was built in three sections, much like the wings on Northrop's smaller single-engine Alpha, Delta, and Gamma transports of the early 1930s. The wing's center section was constructed as part of the fuselage, eliminating the need for the carry-through spars that obstructed the aisle of the Boeing 247. The center section also made possible an additional landing flap under the fuselage that helped the DC-1 comply with TWA's contractual stipulation that it land at 65mph. The concept was so new the flaps were trade-named "Douglas Air Brakes." Having no way of testing such strong wing sec-

Flying by Ear

I remember, for instance, that the fuel selectors made good footrests and were worn down on the edges from years of this use. You had to place your shoe at just the right angle or you would shut off the flow on one side, something we all did while learning the correct technique. Outside of takeoff and landing, or when riding through rough air, the rudder was not needed once the trim was set. The cockpit was, by the standards of that day, quiet and comfortable. The Three was inherently stable and would fly all day hands off, except for one thing—the stewardess walking up and down the aisle. If she moved three feet the nose tried to rise or dip. "Here comes lunch," the man at the controls would say just before the door opened....

Standard airline practice called for a climb to 300 feet above the selected cruising level and a shallow dive to "get her on the step." Increasing air traffic forced us to abandon this procedure and level off exactly on the money, leaving on climb power until the airspeed read a bit more than normal cruise speed. Then you eased the power controls back and maintained that tail high, extra speed configuration indefinitely. Propeller synchronization was obtained manually by working one knob against the other until engine drone was steady. You could tell a great deal about engine health with your ears in such an unpressurized ship. They either sounded right or they didn't, and when they didn't you began paying more attention to engine instruments, checking mags, fooling with engine controls and using such troubleshooting tricks as might pin down the trouble. A long look back at each engine might reveal a roughness not severe enough to travel through the airframe and into the cockpit floor. Oil seeping from beneath the cowl flaps might be the clue, so you developed the knack of making small talk with a passenger without his realizing you were more interested in the engine outside his window.

—Len Morgan, *The Douglas DC-3*

tions, an engineer—the same Fred Herman who accompanied Carl Cover on the DC-1's first flight—drove a steamroller back and forth over one, with no visible effect.

Both of the Museum of Flight's DC-3s flew well into the 1980s, forty-year careers in each case. N138D was built in 1940 for American Airlines as one of 170 long-distance DC-3As with two-row Pratt & Whitney Twin Wasp engines and extended-range fuel tanks. The changes doubled the DC-3's range to 2,125 miles and raised its passenger capacity to thirty. During the early 1980s it was owned by Nevada Air, which used its DC-3s to fly tourists through the Grand Canyon. N138D also ferried Boeing flight test employees to and from the company's test site ninety miles north of Las Vegas. This one has logged nearly 21,000 hours in the air and participated in the DC-3 Fiftieth Anniversary Fly-In at Expo 86.

DC-3-455 N15748 was completed on January 26, 1943, for Eastern Airlines but flew with Inland Airlines crews on behalf of the U.S. Army Air Corps in Alaska into 1944. Starting June 2, 1945, it spent twelve years with Delta Air Lines before ending its first career as a scheduled airliner with North Central Airlines in 1968. It passed through several owners' hands until it was refurbished and bought by Salair Inc., an Alaska and Pacific Northwest short-haul cargo operator founded in 1980 by Joseph Salerno, and was donated by him to the Museum eight years later. N15748 has been restored with help from both McDonnell Douglas Corporation and Alaska Airlines, whose early postwar colors it carries.

The DC-3 was the first airplane to support itself in the air financially as well as mechanically. Dwight Eisenhower called the DC-3's military version, the C-47, one of the four decisive weapons in the Allied victory in World War II, along with the jeep, the bazooka, and the atom bomb. The C-47 was so useful even the Germans and the Japanese had them. The Soviets flew more than 2,000 license-built copies, which were called Lisunov Li-2s.

"It is my feeling, as an interested observer during the entire lifespan of this airplane," DC-3 airline copilot Len Morgan wrote in 1966, "that the DC-3 is the most important airplane ever built."

DOUGLAS DC-3

Dimensions

Overall wingspan 95ft

Overall length 64ft 6in

Height 16ft 11in

Engines

Two Pratt & Whitney R-1830, 1,200hp

Weight

Empty 16,865lbs

Loaded 25,200lbs

Performance

Maximum speed 230mph

Cruise 207mph

Range (DC-3A) 2,125mi

Service ceiling 18,000ft

Boeing B-17F Flying Fortress

Few warplanes have reached such timely developmental peaks as the Boeing B-17 Flying Fortress bomber. First flown July 28, 1935, and the only four-engine bomber in the U.S. Army Air Corps' inventory in 1937, it was also the only first-line combat aircraft to retain that status throughout World War II. The B-17's longevity was rare and underlines the farsightedness of its original design.

Yet it became an effective weapon only in 1942, and it was not until 1943 and the introduction of long-range escort fighters in Europe that it became a war-winning weapon. By early 1945 it was replaced in the Pacific by Boeing's phenomenal B-29 for long-range missions. That heyday, however brief, was so perfectly timed that the Fort will long merit its own chapter in the annals of aerial warfare.

The Flying Fortress was there at the moment it was needed most because Boeing's top management and engineers, including the great Edward C. Wells, anticipated each step in the evolution of strategic bombing. Speed came

Above: Centerpiece of the Museum of Flight's collection, this B-17F is the oldest airworthy Flying Fortress in the world. *Right*: Most surviving B-17s are, like this one, B-17Gs. The G traded speed for armament: not much of a loss since massed formations of B-17s seldom flew at more than 180mph over Occupied Europe.

first: early models could do 300 miles per hour. Then came altitude: supercharged engines took the B-17 past 25,000 feet. Bigger flying surfaces on the B-17E made it a stable bombing platform for pinpoint accuracy in daylight.

From the beginning, the B-17 was a beautiful aircraft, and the B-17F of 1942 was arguably the best-looking Flying Fortress of all; less heavily armed than the definitive G model, it looked sleeker. The Museum of Flight's airplane is a B-17F, the oldest Fort still flying of the 12,731 built.

One hallmark of Boeing design has been careful evolution through many design studies, culminating, when conditions are right, in seemingly revolutionary breakthroughs. The B-17's origins lay in three previous Boeing designs that were too advanced for their own good.

The Model 200 Monomail of 1930 used the same engine as Boeing's Model 40B mail/express biplane, but could cruise effortlessly at 135mph—more than the biplane's top speed—using only sixty percent power. The difference was made by aerodynamic refinements: retractable landing gear, a single internally braced wing, and all-metal construction. The YB-9 bomber of 1931 was a twin-engine derivative of the Monomail that was actually faster than contemporary fighters, but lost the production contract it was designed to win. Only seven YB-9s were built.

In 1933 the B-9's peaceful offspring, the 200mph Boeing 247 airliner, caused such a sensation coming into exclusive service with United Air Lines that the competition was forced to commission Douglas Aircraft to come up with something better: the immortal DC-1, -2, and -3 series. Boeing built only seventy-five 247s.

By mid-1934 it seemed that, as progressive as the company had become, Boeing was in no position to build anything as ambitious as a four-engine bomber. Under new antitrust laws, William Boeing's United Aircraft & Transport, consisting of both airplane manufacturers and airlines,

Wartime mass production of the B-17 made the Boeing Company an aviation colossus. Boeing produced the first batch of service-test YIB-17s at a loss; several years later the bomber was being produced by three companies in several plants.

was ordered broken up. The $3 million 247 sale to United Air Lines had been Boeing's biggest so far, but that money was gone. In January 1934, 1,700 people had worked at Boeing; by May that number plunged to 900, on its way to 600.

The same month, though, Boeing was invited to design a single XBLR-1 (Experimental Bomber, Long-Range, Number One) for the U.S. Army Air Corps. It would be the largest U.S. land-based bomber yet built, with five times the range of the B-9 and B-10. The contract for what became the Model 294, or XB-15, as it was later designated, was worth $600,000. The plane was so advanced it didn't fly until 1937, partly because no engines of sufficient power were available. But its wing found its way onto the dozen Boeing 314 Clipper flying boats. Its four-engine technology eventually made Boeing "World Center of 4-Engine Airplane Development," as the company advertised on a billboard overlooking Boeing Field, south of Seattle, in 1941.

In August 1934, the Air Corps announced it wanted a multiengine bomber that would carry a bombload of 2,000 pounds over 1,020 miles (but with a desired range of 2,200 miles) at 200mph (but with a desired top speed of 250mph). There would be no money up front. It had to be ready for testing in a year. The prize: an order for 220 airplanes!

On September 26, 1934, the board of directors of the newly independent Boeing Airplane Company voted $275,000 for design work on the Model 299. Boeing designs are team efforts: seventy-three engineers worked around the clock, seven days a week, for three weeks doing the basic design. One of them was Ed Wells, a 24-year-old engineering honors graduate of Stanford who had worked on the tail surfaces of the 247. By the time the shape of the new bomber had emerged, so had Wells as its principal draftsman. In 1935, only four years after joining Boeing, Wells was assistant project engineer on the B-17, under E. Gifford Emery.

A Boeing worker finishes the front office of a B-17G. One G-model identifying characteristic is the chin turret, which helped correct a long-standing weakness of the Fort: its susceptibility to a head-on attack.

DESIGNER: EDWARD C. WELLS

Very few outside of Seattle or the aviation industry have heard of the late Edward C. Wells. That was his style, and it became Boeing's. Designing and building airplanes has always been a team game at Boeing, and no single individual stood for Boeing's team approach as well as Wells did. He was involved with every Boeing design from the 247 on and held patents on all of them.

Although their sheer size usually attracted most of the attention, it was the wings on Boeing designs that were most consistently outstanding. Wells was Boeing's wing man for forty-one years, and that made him the company's "Number One Engineer" from 1935, when the B-17 first flew, to the appearance of the 747 jumbo jet in 1969.

Since he was head of Boeing's preliminary design unit by 1936, chief engineer by 1943, and vice president of engineering just four years later, Wells had more influence, for a longer period of time, on more important aircraft, than any American aircraft designer ever. After he retired in 1972, he remained as a kind of chief engineer emeritus with the company for the next six critical years, when Boeing's current models were being developed.

When Wells started out with Boeing, his specialty was flaps. Flaps were fairly new in 1935. That year Boeing became the first American company to fit flaps to fighters, when they were retrofitted to the U.S. Army Air Corps'

fleet of Boeing P-26 fighters, designed by then-chief engineer Charles N. Montieth. These, the first American monoplane fighters, were considered too hot to handle, touching down at 82mph. The flaps were quite sophisticated for their time: recessed into the underside wing skin, dropped by hand-cranking to forty-five degrees, they lowered the P-26's landing speed by a critical 9mph.

The single design most closely identified with Wells is Boeing's Model 299, the B-17 prototype, which flew the same year. In his book *Vision*, Harold Mansfield, a Boeing executive at the time, tells how Monty Montieth thought the flaps Wells was drawing for the Model 299 were too large.

"Let's don't stretch our luck," Mansfield quotes Montieth as saying to Wells. "Leave the flaps off. We'll have good brakes." Wells produced wind-tunnel data that showed the Model 299 would be able to take off with 2,000lbs more payload with flaps than without. His influence over the airplane's development increased as it got better. The B-17B, for example, featured a larger rudder and flaps.

Although by 1935 flaps were appearing on almost all new designs, they were enough of a novelty for companies to patent or assign trade names to their flap systems. The flaps on the Douglas DC-3 were called "Douglas Air

Brakes." Lockheed introduced slotted Fowler flaps that unfold in sections, adding to wing area as well as curvature. Wells's B-17 flaps were the biggest ever in 1935, and Boeing surpassed the competition in building bigger wings, for bigger airplanes, with all these features.

Throughout Boeing's ascendant period leading to the 747, Wells made key configuration decisions on each new design. He drew the optimal pressurized fuselage cross section, a perfect circle, for the Stratoliner, which already had his B-17 wings and tail. He outlined the super-slick aerodynamic requirements for the B-29, which became the most complicated single piece of machinery ever devised up to 1943 in the effort to minimize the drag of its gun turrets and engine nacelles. It, too, had a circular cross section. The B-29's airliner derivative, the Stratocruiser, had a two-deck, double-bubble fuselage, in order to modify that circular cross section into a roomier and deeper fuselage profile.

In these instances the interaction between civil and military types was direct: whole systems from one appeared on the other. With the B-47 Stratojet bomber, one side set the mold for the other. The B-47 showed what the big jet would look like, and in the series of jetliners that ensued, every model was better than the last.

By this time Wells was making very basic choices about the layouts of future Boeing aircraft. As successful as the Boeings of the B-17 to B-47 period were under Wells's direct influence, every major design that has appeared since has been better, both operationally and in the marketplace. The more general Wells's influence became, the better Boeing's products became. His was the primary engineering hand in the development of the Boeing 707, the first successful jet airliner.

One of the most difficult of many such choices was Wells's decision to support the unpopular three-engine layout (advocated by George Steiner) for the 727. He also supervised the development of its revolutionary wing, very small in area for clean cruising while able to add more than twenty-five percent for low-speed takeoffs and landings, using triple-slotted flaps and leading-edge slats and spoilers. These lift-enhancement devices made the 727 "the airplane whose wing comes apart." By 1982 it had become the best-selling jetliner of all time at nearly 2,000 copies.

That wing became the basis for the wing design on the 747. In addition, the 747's trademark wide-body flow-through cross section with upper-deck bubble came from an Ed Wells decision to drop an earlier full-length double-bubble two-deck design. Wells killed a proposal to repeat a design feature that he himself had introduced on the Stratocruiser, in favor of a shape somewhat reminiscent of the B-17's.

During his near-half-century with Boeing, Wells accumulated twenty patents, the last of which was for the landing gear system on the Boeing 767. In engineering terms, his amazing career stretched from designing the tail surfaces for the Boeing 247 airliner through overseeing the Minuteman intercontinental ballistic missile program, to development of the X-20 Dyna-Soar, father of today's Space Shuttle.

Wells won every important aviation-industry honor available to him: the 1942 Lawrence Sperry Award from the Institute of the Aeronautical Sciences for his contribution to the design of four-engine aircraft; the 1944 Fawcett Aviation Award; the 1980 Daniel Guggenheim Medal for "outstanding contributions in the design and production of some of the world's most famous military and commercial aircraft." In 1985, he won the Tony Janus Award for his contributions to complex aerospace systems.

On Wells's death at seventy-five, Boeing chairman T. A. Wilson said, "There's no question he was the company's outstanding engineer during his long career. The technical organizations at Boeing revered him and his talent."

Facing page: Quiet, studious Edward C. Wells was Boeing's "Number 1 Engineer" for most of 41 years.

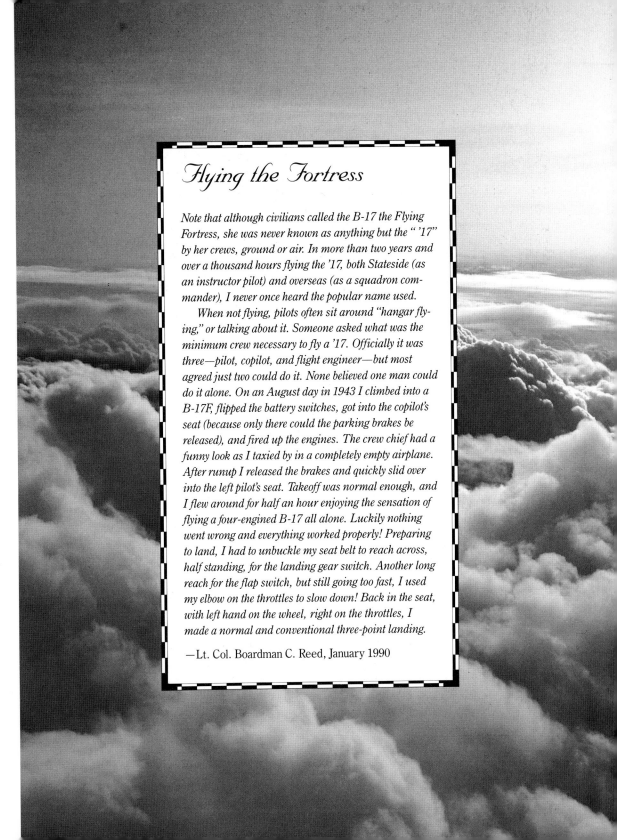

Flying the Fortress

Note that although civilians called the B-17 the Flying Fortress, she was never known as anything but the " '17" by her crews, ground or air. In more than two years and over a thousand hours flying the '17, both Stateside (as an instructor pilot) and overseas (as a squadron commander), I never once heard the popular name used.

When not flying, pilots often sit around "hangar flying," or talking about it. Someone asked what was the minimum crew necessary to fly a '17. Officially it was three—pilot, copilot, and flight engineer—but most agreed just two could do it. None believed one man could do it alone. On an August day in 1943 I climbed into a B-17F, flipped the battery switches, got into the copilot's seat (because only there could the parking brakes be released), and fired up the engines. The crew chief had a funny look as I taxied by in a completely empty airplane. After runup I released the brakes and quickly slid over into the left pilot's seat. Takeoff was normal enough, and I flew around for half an hour enjoying the sensation of flying a four-engined B-17 all alone. Luckily nothing went wrong and everything worked properly! Preparing to land, I had to unbuckle my seat belt to reach across, half standing, for the landing gear switch. Another long reach for the flap switch, but still going too fast, I used my elbow on the throttles to slow down! Back in the seat, with left hand on the wheel, right on the throttles, I made a normal and conventional three-point landing.

—Lt. Col. Boardman C. Reed, January 1990

A P-38 Lightning fighter, the bomber crews' "little friend," leaves this formation of B-17Fs and Gs in early 1943. The P-38 was the first fighter to accompany American heavy bombers deep into Germany.

An important factor in any company-financed aircraft project is the cost of the engines. Although the term "multiengine" was understood at the time to mean two, Boeing's engineers wanted four. To them, four engines meant more speed: an estimated 235mph for the new bomber. The size and number of defensive gun positions on the Model 299, as Boeing designated the B-17 prototype, made one newspaperman gasp that this was "a veritable flying fortress" when it was rolled out for its first flight on July 28, 1935.

Test pilot Leslie Tower and three others flew the 299 from Seattle to the Army's test center at Wright Field, Dayton, Ohio, on August 20. Two thousand miles nonstop, in exactly nine hours, at an average 233mph—unheard-of figures. Tower and the 299 did this on sixty-three percent power. When the crew arrived, they were greeted by Boeing president Clairmont Egtvedt and Ed Wells. Bud Benton, the head mechanic, climbed out of the plane and asked why so few people were there for this historic event.

"You're not supposed to be here," Wells replied. "Claire and I estimated you'd be due an hour from now. The field expects you in two or three."

Boeing's Model 299 was the star of the Army's 1935 three-plane flyoff for the bomber contract. It easily outperformed the Douglas and Martin entries, and could carry eight 600lb bombs internally. Tower was aboard the 299 one morning in October when an Army pilot, Maj. Pete Hill, fired it up, took off, flew straight up, then fell off on one wing and started to straighten out before crashing.

Hill had forgotten to release the locks that held the Model 299's flying surfaces rigid on the ground. No previous military aircraft had required wind-gust locks for its control surfaces; no plane had been so big the wind could damage its rudder and elevators. The 299 had taken off with them locked and was therefore uncontrollable. Hill died that afternoon. Tower, disconsolate at having allowed it to happen, died soon after from his burns. The Douglas B-18, a recog-

Fighters at Nine O'Clock

We were perhaps a little off course. I could see the Weser as it wound south of Bremerhaven, off the starboard wing, guiding us to Bremen.

A squawk from someone: "Fighters at nine o'clock." I rested my gun on the desk to note developments and saw that the gun was making a grease puddle on the log and the maps. The word "fighters" scrawled its way through the stain.

The convulsion of the [upper] turret gun blasting over my head filled the nose. I stopped writing and picked up my gun. The fighters coming in were each an inch of silver against the blue. They came in three abreast at three o'clock above the frosty patterns on the port-side window. The wings grew to two or three inches and touched off little sparklers. Then they were no longer inches but massive aircraft, flipping over, spitting, and sliding down out of my gunsights, like gulls gliding down currents of air to the dull metallic sheen of the distant earth.

I pulled the trigger and sent a long burst into space. Tondelayo, in evasive action, seemed to jump and fall so that much of the time I was standing in air seeking to steady myself on the handlebars of my gun....

... From my vantage point I saw them only when they came head on, flashing, turning and exiting in marvelous choreography. The impersonal quality of the menace was eerie. It was as if we were in battle with beautiful birds of prey....

I saw death long before I saw pain, and I could not believe it. I balanced my gun in one hand and stared beyond it at Carlson's left-wing man. Was it Johnson? Was it Ashley? I no longer remember....

... In the arctic chill my forehead dripped sweat onto my brows and my nose. I had just pulled aside the elephantine hose of my oxygen mask to tally the dimly seen curves of the Weser with those on my map when I heard an unfamiliar noise like the crunch of metal. Simultaneously I felt that someone had brushed against my helmet, knocking it slightly awry.

White fleecy cotton padding was fluttering around me as if a playful cat had ripped a pillow. Bob turned to me, and his eyes above the mask were clouded with concern. I waved cheerily, then followed his eyes to a jagged hole in the metal frame beneath the window. There Tondelayo's skin had curled inward. I looked behind me to where the cat had ripped the pillow and followed the bullet's course to where it had exited above and behind me into the wadding that cushioned the bulkhead. Bob gestured to my helmet and I let my fingers trace the bullet's path in the groove that now creased the tin....

—Elmer Bendiner, *The Fall of Fortresses*

nizably inferior design that mated DC-2 wings and tail to a beer-belly fuselage, won the contract. But the Model 299 had been so impressive, despite the crash, that Boeing was authorized to build thirteen Y1B-17s (Y for test) and a fourteenth for strength testing.

That extra aircraft, never intended for flight, was eventually used to flight-test the turbo-superchargers installed on subsequent models. The supercharged Wright Cyclone engines took the B-17 up to 30,000 feet, an altitude at which, in 1936, a bomber would be untouchable. It was the first of seven models' worth of constant development that lasted through World War II.

By 1941, when twenty B-17C Fortresses were supplied to the Royal Air Force, the basic design was at its peak speed—well over 300mph. But it was by no means ready for war. Although the RAF's 90 Squadron operated their B-17s with valor, they lost half their strength between July and September.

Boeing realized the B-17 was not yet combat-ready even before the RAF proved it. With hundreds of engineer-

Five Grand, the 5,000th B-17 built in Seattle since Pearl Harbor, is shown on its mid-1944 test flight, autographed for the occasion by the men and women who built it.

ing changes, the most obvious of them the huge fin that made the Fort into the plane its pilots affectionately called the "Big-Assed Bird," as well as new turrets above the cockpit, in the belly, and in the tail, the B-17E flew September 5, 1941. It was seven tons heavier than the Model 299 and forty percent faster. The E was a long step in the right direction, but it took more time yet to perfect the first Flying Fortresses fit to fight.

Although outwardly it looked much like the E, the B-17F had more than 400 additional internal modifications, including more powerful engines and paddle-bladed propellers for more thrust at higher altitudes, and a better oxygen system to help the crew withstand those heights. The main outward clue to an F was its clear, one-piece nose bubble, which improved the bombardier's view from the plane. The F began to be produced in April 1942 and was the first B-17 model to be turned out by Boeing in Seattle, by Lockheed's Vega plant in Burbank, and by Douglas at Long Beach simultaneously.

The B-17F at the Museum of Flight has survived careers as an Eighth Air Force bomber during the spring of 1944 in England; as a static war memorial in Arkansas; as an aerial sprayer bombing Lansing, Michigan, with DDT in 1953; and, finally, as a fire-bomber until 1985, when it was bought by Seattle's Bob Richardson to become the centerpiece of the Museum's collection. It was a star in the 1968 movie *The Thousand Bomber Raid* and the 1969 epic *Tora! Tora! Tora!* and flew to England during the summer of 1989 to appear in the movie *Memphis Belle* with five other flyable B-17s. Repainted in its wartime olive-drab-and-gray camouflage, it had a supporting role as "C-Cup," carrying appropriately bosomy nose art.

Despite a normal bombload smaller than many other Allied bomber types (normal bombload, 4,000–5,000lbs), the Flying Fortress dropped 640,036 tons of bombs on European targets (compared with 452,508 tons by B-24 Liberators and 463,544 tons by all other aircraft).

From late 1942 to late 1944 it had been a decisive factor in the Allied victory in Europe. By 1945 the B-17 was obsolete as a frontline bomber. The job was done.

BOEING B-17F FLYING FORTRESS

Dimensions

Overall wingspan 103ft 9½in

Overall length (tail up) 74ft 9in

Height (tail down) 19ft 1in

Engines

Four Wright R-1820-97 engines,
1,200hp at 25,000ft, 1,380hp in
"war emergency" power at 25,000ft

Weight

Empty 34,000lbs

Loaded (maximum) 65,500lbs

Defensive armament . . . . 11 .50-caliber machine guns

Normal bombload 4,000lbs

Maximum bombload 13,600lbs

Performance

Maximum speed 299mph

Cruising speed 200mph

Service ceiling 37,500ft

Range (with 6,000lb bombs,
  at 10,000ft) . . . . 1,300mi at 200mph

Crew 10

The Wildcat evolved from biplane to monoplane while on the
drawing board. Nevertheless, it had a certain grace in the air.

General Motors FM-2 Wildcat

The tubby Grumman F4F Wildcat was the most underrated American fighter of World War II. Although it achieved mass production after losing the competition it was built for, it lacked range in the vast Pacific, and it was officially acknowledged as inferior in performance to its principal opponent, the Mitsubishi A6M "Zero."

But although this ugly duckling is generally considered to have been mediocre during its active career, its record of shooting down seven enemy aircraft for each Wildcat loss is an argument to the contrary. Its weaknesses were minimized by teamwork among the Wildcat's pilots, and its strengths made it the only naval fighter to remain in first-line service throughout the war. The difference between failure and success often has less to do with the state of the technology than with how that technology is used.

The U.S. Navy Bureau of Aeronautics (BuAer) had finally decided to make the switch from biplane to monoplane fighters in 1935, and ordered a monoplane design from Brewster Aeronautical Corporation, a neighbor of Grumman Aircraft Engineering on Long Island. As a hedge, in 1936 BuAer also asked Grumman to draw up a successor to its F3F biplane fighter, then coming into service as the main fleet defense fighter. William T. Schwendler, Grumman's chief engineer, went to work on a smaller, faster biplane, the XF4F-1. (X for experimental, F4 for the fourth fighter type from Grumman, whose BuAer manufacturer's code was the letter F. The suffix -1 indicated the first model of the original design.)

Brewster had been a custom car-body builder since early in the century, installing coachwork on American-built Rolls-Royce chassis, then moved into airplane subcontracting in 1932 and produced a highly regarded monoplane dive-bomber, the XSBA-1 (SB for scout bomber, A for Brewster). It was ordered in 1934 and flew in 1936. The credibility of Brewster's designer, Dayton T. Brown, was thus established with BuAer. The F2A (or Buffalo, as the British named it) was a disappointment when first delivered in early 1938, but wind-tunnel tests at Langley, Virginia, indicated that changes to the engine cowling and air intakes would yield dramatic improvements.

Meanwhile, Grumman's Schwendler was projecting that, even with the new 800-horsepower radials from either Wright or Pratt & Whitney, his new design number G-16 biplane would do only 264 miles per hour, barely 10mph faster than the F3F. By mutual agreement between Grumman and BuAer, the contract was canceled, and no XF4F-1 was ever built.

Schwendler then converted his biplane to a midwing monoplane, splitting the difference by putting the single wing halfway up the fuselage on design number G-18. Although Grumman got a later start than Brewster, the XF4F-2 flew three months before the XF2A, on September 2, 1937. The test pilot was Robert L. Hall.

The F4F-2 prototype still looked odd, with rounded tips on all its flying surfaces and a strange forward-sloping rudder. In a flyoff with the Brewster entry and a modified version of the Army's Seversky P-35, the F4F was fastest at 292mph but kept overheating in the air. The Brewster F2A was declared winner of the early-1938 naval fighter contest, but BuAer allowed Grumman to continue development of the Wildcat, as the plane had been named by Grumman. Since then, all mass-produced Grumman fighters have been named for cats, and they have become the most successful line of naval fighter planes in the world.

The next version, the XF4F-3, had squared-off wingtips and tail surfaces, a 1,200hp, two-stage supercharged engine for better high-altitude performance, and four additional feet of wingspan. The XF4F-3 reached 334mph in service testing during the spring of 1939, and an order for fifty-four was forthcoming that August. The shape and size of the Wildcat was set.

A total of 7,898 were built from 1940 to 1945, more than half of them by General Motors' Eastern Aircraft Divi-

F4F-3 Wildcats on the deck of USS *Enterprise* in early 1942. The first of many changes in markings to instantly differentiate American warplanes from their opponents in combat was the application of the largest possible markings, some of which did not quite cover the previous ones. Soon the red disks were ordered deleted from the centers of the stars, a process barely under way here.

sion. The Museum of Flight's exhibit is one of these, an FM-2 (M for Eastern Aircraft, -2 for the second Wildcat version Eastern built) with more power, a taller fin to handle the increased output, and a lightened airframe—the ultimate Wildcat. Nothing is known of its service history, partly because most of the clues were destroyed during its ten years as a playground hulk outside Seattle.

The single design feature that made the Wildcat unique was its ridiculous-looking hand-cranked retractable landing gear, a Rube Goldberg assemblage of sprockets, bicycle chains, and a dozen hinged struts, all of which folded into a bay behind the engine. Like the airplane itself, the landing gear's only virtues were its rugged reliability and, despite all the parts, its fundamental simplicity.

This landing gear was the first product of the Grumman company, which was founded December 5, 1929. It grew out of a company headed by America's first formally trained aeronautical engineer, Grover Loening, who had worked for the Wright brothers before starting his plane-making business in a New York City loft in 1917. In October 1920, Loening persuaded Lt. Leroy Randle Grumman to leave the Navy, signing him on as test pilot and plant manager. Four years later Loening recruited the two other young men who would be key personalities at Grumman, Leon "Jake" Swirbul and Schwendler.

Loening sold his company in 1928, and Grumman, Swirbul, and Schwendler decided to start their own firm, pooling $58,825 to capitalize it. Loening was an initial investor, and former Loening employees were hand-picked to join the new Grumman Aircraft Engineering Corporation.

Their first work consisted of repairing Loening seaplanes. All Navy Loenings were amphibians, and the Navy was anxious to make the rest of its seaplanes amphibious as well. During his last few months with Loening, Grumman designed a retractable landing gear that would fit into existing seaplane floats. That basic design was in continuous production until 1945, when the last Wildcats came off the line.

 Schwendler's lasting contribution to Grumman was the "Schwendler Factor." Among the many types created by Grumman, the world's leading producer of naval aircraft, the

Grumman F4F Wildcat

Interchangeability keeps 'em flying

Unit construction and interchangeability helped put many a needed fighter

back in the air again in the early touch-and-go days at Henderson Field.

Emergency change of damaged blades, frequently found necessary in the midst of battle,

is typical of the quick replacement possible through the Curtiss Electric's unit construction.

CURTISS ELECTRIC PROPELLERS

Curtiss unit construction
permits compact shipment

Curtiss-Wright Corporation, Propeller Division

Wildcat exemplifies the company's unique design philosophy. Briefly stated, the Schwendler Factor was the notion that if something was strong enough according to the specifications, it wouldn't hurt to make it twice as strong. Keeping their designs simple and strong put Grumman among America's handful of elite high-tech companies and has kept them there ever since.

Because Leroy Grumman was an introvert, Swirbul became the company's most visible face. He may have been the most enlightened wartime aircraft plant manager in the United States. Swirbul built a work force that was one-third women and included 800 blacks. Women worked in most wartime industries, but at Grumman they became aircraft captains and test pilots. Blacks were introduced into the plant, despite overt hostility on the shop floor, by means of Swirbul's recruiting a much-admired local black basketball star, putting him through training school, and making him an inspector.

The result, aside from simultaneous volume production of six different combat aircraft types during World War II, was a steadily declining cost per airplane that moved the Navy to assert after the war that Grumman had produced more pounds of airframe for the taxpayer's dollar than any other company.

As for Leroy Grumman, his self-effacement set a pattern of happy employee relations at the company. Off by himself, Roy, as he was known in the plant, was capable of finding ingenious, straightforward solutions to engineering

Wildcats also served as Atlantic Convoy escorts and advanced trainers.

Matched Turn for Turn

"Never dogfight with a Zero," new Navy fighter pilots were told when they arrived in the South Pacific. But there have been many instances of great pilots equalizing the differences between their machines. One such American pilot is memorialized by Saburo Sakai, a leading Japanese ace, in one of the classic accounts of air-to-air combat:

Finally I saw them, about 1,500 feet below me. I gaped. A single Wildcat pursued three Zero fighters, firing in short bursts at the frantic Japanese planes. All four planes were in a wild dogfight, flying tight left spirals. The Zeros should have been able to take the lone Grumman without any trouble, but every time a Zero caught the Wildcat before its guns the enemy plane flipped away wildly and came out again on the tail of a Zero. I had never seen such flying before.

I banked my wings to signal Sasai and dove. The Wildcat was clinging grimly to the tail of a Zero, its tracers chewing up the wings and tail. In desperation I snapped out a burst. At once the Grumman snapped away in a roll to the right, clawed around in a tight turn, and ended up in a climb straight at my own plane. Never had I seen an enemy plane move so quickly or so gracefully before; and every second his guns were moving closer to the belly of my fighter. I snap-rolled in an effort to throw him off. He would not be shaken. He was using my own favorite tactics, coming up from under.

I chopped the throttle back and the Zero shuddered as its speed fell. It worked; his timing off, the enemy pilot pulled back in a turn. I slammed the throttle forward again, rolling to the left. Three times I rolled the Zero, then dropped in a spin, and came out in a left vertical spiral. The Wildcat matched me turn for turn. Our left

wings both pointed at a right angle to the sea below us, the right wings at the sky.

Neither of us could gain an advantage. We held to the spiral, tremendous G pressures pushing us down in our seats with every passing second. My heart pounded wildly, and my head felt as if it weighed a ton. A gray film seemed to be clouding over my eyes. I gritted my teeth; if the enemy pilot could take the punishment, so could I. The man who failed first and turned in any other direction to ease the pressure would be finished.

On the fifth spiral, the Wildcat skidded slightly. I had him, I thought. But the Grumman dropped its nose, gained speed, and the pilot again had his plane under full control. There was a terrific man behind that stick.

He made his error, however, in the next moment. Instead of swinging back to go into a sixth spiral, he fed power to his engine, broke away at an angle, and looped. That was the decisive split second. I went right after him, cutting inside the Grumman's arc, and came out on his tail. I had him. He kept flying loops, trying to narrow down the distance of each arc. Every time he went up and around I cut inside his arc and lessened the distance between our two planes. The Zero could outfly any fighter in the world in this kind of maneuver.

When I was only fifty yards away, the Wildcat broke out of his loop and astonished me by flying straight and level. At this distance I would not need the cannon; I pumped 200 rounds into the Grumman's cockpit, watching the bullets chew up the thin metal skin and shattering the glass.

I could not believe what I saw; the Wildcat continued flying almost as if nothing had happened. A Zero which had taken that many bullets into its vital cockpit would

have been a ball of fire by now. I could not understand it. I slammed the throttle forward and closed in to the American plane, just as the enemy fighter lost speed. In a moment I was ten yards ahead of the Wildcat, trying to slow down. I hunched my shoulders, prepared for the onslaught of his guns. I was trapped.

No bullets came. The Wildcat's guns remained silent. The entire situation was unbelievable. I dropped my speed until our planes were flying wing-to-wing formation. I opened my cockpit window and stared out. The Wildcat's cockpit canopy was already back, and I could see the pilot clearly. He was a big man, with a round face. He wore a light khaki uniform. He appeared to be middle-aged, not as young as I had expected.

For several seconds we flew along in our bizarre formation, our eyes meeting across the narrow space between the two planes. The Wildcat was a shambles. Bullet holes had cut the fuselage and wings up from one end to the other. The skin of the rudder was gone, and the metal ribs stuck out like a skeleton. Now I could understand his horizontal flight, and also why the pilot had not fired. Blood stained his right shoulder, and I saw the dark patch moving downward over his chest. It was incredible that his plane was still in the air.

But this was no way to kill a man! Not with him flying helplessly, wounded, his plane a wreck. I raised my left hand and shook my fist at him, shouting, uselessly, I know, for him to fight instead of flying along like a clay pigeon. The American looked startled; he raised his right hand weakly and waved.

—Saburo Sakai, with Martin Caidin and Fred Saito, *Samurai!*

problems. The folding landing gear for amphibians was an early example. The Wildcat, using that same undercarriage, had no hydraulic systems to leak and fail in combat. Its flaps were operated by vacuum from the engine, and its landing gear was raised and lowered manually by a crank on the right-hand console. The crank took twenty-one revolutions, which explains the Wildcat's roller-coaster full-power climb-out from carriers: the pilot, cranking like mad, could not help moving the stick back and forth with each turn.

Fooling around with a straightened paper clip and a pink gum eraser, Roy Grumman produced the company's patented wing-folding system. An inclined single hinge enabled the Wildcat's wing to fold back along the fuselage, instead of upward as on most carrier-borne aircraft. In the confined spaces of below-deck carrier hangars, where aircraft could only be hung from the ceiling to get them out of the way, the Grumman hinge made a real difference. The Wildcat stayed in production until 1945 because it was the only naval fighter small enough to operate from smaller escort carriers.

Under the conditions of war in the Pacific before Midway, almost any fighter being flown purely defensively and by green pilots would have fared poorly against the seasoned Japanese in their fast, maneuverable Zero fighters. But the Wildcat held the line. At Wake Island, the Marine garrison held out for fifteen days as the four patched-up Wildcats that survived the Japanese attack routed one invasion force and held off another, until the weight of numbers doomed the defenders.

New tactics emphasizing teamwork were developed to capitalize on the Wildcat's ruggedness. Lt. Edward "Butch" O'Hare, after whom Chicago's international airport is named, shot down five Mitsubishi "Betty" bombers in four minutes flying an early-model Wildcat on the afternoon of February 20, 1942. Maj. Joseph Foss, the Marines' leading ace, shot down all twenty-six of his victims from Wildcats—and would have had many more had he spent as much time fighting the enemy as he did malaria.

From America's entry into the war until August 1943, the Grumman Wildcat was the only fighter the Navy had to face the Zero. It was enough.

Dimensions

Overall wingspan 38ft

Overall length 28ft 10in

Height 11ft 11in

Engine

One Wright R-1820-56 Cyclone 9-cylinder radial, 1,350hp

Weight

Empty 5,448lbs

Loaded 8,271lbs

(compared with F4F-4, FM-1: 5,785lbs and 7,952lbs)

Performance

Maximum speed 332mph

Initial climb . . . . more than 2,000ft/min

Range (typical) 900mi

Service ceiling (early versions, less with FM-2) 35,000ft

Facing page: Leroy Grumman's ingenious folding-wing design minimized the width of space his planes occupied in the crowded below-decks carrier hangar. *This page*: The Grumman XF4F-3 "Fighting Plane" prototype shows its streamlined propeller spinner, only two guns in the nose, and telescopic gunsight, visible evidence that the Grumman design, though a vast improvement over the Navy's first-line equipment in 1939, was not yet ready for war.

Goodyear FG-1 Corsair

"The Corsair was the first of several planes to come out during the middle of the war," Greg "Pappy" Boyington, its most famous pilot, recalled in an interview in 1984, forty-four years after the Corsair first flew. "It was the first 400-mile-per-hour, fully loaded military plane. It replaced the Wildcat and was a big improvement. You couldn't outclimb the Japanese with the Wildcat, and they were faster than you and could outturn you. The Corsair was a sweet-flying baby if I ever flew one. It could climb with a Zero, only with a more shallow angle of climb, and it had considerably more speed. With the Corsair, we could make our own rules."

The Chance Vought Corporation's design group, headed by Rex Beisel, responded to a 1938 U.S. Navy Bureau of Aeronautics (BuAer) call for a fighter design that would match the performance of the best land-based fighters. It was a challenging request, and Beisel replied with a design that was conventional in concept but daring in detail.

Beisel's design process started right at the front end. The idea was to put the smallest possible airframe behind the most powerful engine then under development: Pratt & Whitney's massive R-2800 Double Wasp, a fourteen-cylinder two-row radial then promising 1,850 horsepower for takeoff.

(The liquid-cooled engines that powered the principal opponents in the Battle of Britain, two years later, put out 1,030hp.)

To translate all that horsepower into speed, Vought planned to use the largest-diameter propeller ever used on a fighter up to that time: a 13-foot-4-inch Hamilton Standard. The fact that this advanced engine and propeller were coming from within the United Aircraft group, of which Vought was an affiliate, gave Beisel and his team an edge over competing companies—the edge Vought needed to get into the naval fighter business for good.

It was quite an edge. Although it took time to harness all that power to carrier decks, the F4U/FG/F3A Corsairs were the most capable seaborne fighters of their time and rank among the greatest combat aircraft in history.

The Corsair was instrumental in turning the tide of war in the South Pacific, becoming the "Sweetheart of Okinawa" to grateful grunts on the ground and "Whispering Death" to the Japanese. Once the plane's blind, rebounding landing tendencies were tamed, it became unquestionably the best carrier fighter of World War II, achieving an eleven-to-one victory ratio. It was the only American piston-engined fighter still in production during the Korean War.

The big prop and the torque it generated presented most of the problems the Corsair had to address. Beisel's solution, an inverted gull wing, had all the elegance of the best aeronautical engineering. Gull wings had been used before, notably on the German Stuka dive-bombers. On the Corsair, they solved a couple of problems and had some beneficial side effects.

First, the gull wings gave the Corsair's big propeller adequate ground clearance in the tail-up takeoff attitude by simultaneously putting the fuselage up high and landing gear mountings closer to the ground. A bonus was a wing-root joint that was perpendicular to the lower fuselage cross section that gave better airflow. The inverted wing stubs housed oil and supercharger intercooler vents.

Once the exact position of the cockpit was worked out, the gull wings offered better downward vision. The cockpit was moved backward three feet on the production models from its position in the prototype. European combat experience led the design team to install six machine guns in the Corsair's wings, thus displacing the wing tanks; the fuel went where the cockpit had been. The new cockpit location traded away visibility on takeoff and landing for better vision downward in the air. An operational payoff came on ground-

Despite being the first U.S. fighter to exceed 400mph in level flight, the XF4U-1 needed many changes to become perhaps the best carrier fighter in history. Guns went to the wings, wing fuel tanks to the fuselage, cockpit three feet back to make room for the tank.

Goodyear NFG-1D Corsairs at Sand Point Naval Air Station, 1949. The letter N in their designation indicates the aircraft are serving with Naval Reserve squadrons. The Museum of Flight Corsair could be in this picture.

New Qualities of Beauty and Danger

Charles Lindbergh's first impression of the Corsair was no different from that of most pilots. It looked lethal—perhaps as much for its pilot as the opposition. But it had that terrible beauty that so many great weapons embody....

... Ever since my ears heard the noises of daybreak, all things around me—the air I breathe, the ground I walk on, the very trees of the jungle—seem to have taken on new qualities of beauty and danger.

There was the graceful curve of my fighter's wing, as I climbed into the cockpit before takeoff, testifying to the godlike creativeness of man. There was the awkward bulk of my pistol, digging into my chest, reminding me of our satanical destructiveness. I watched the bunched heads of coconut palms streaming past as my land gear retracted and my air speed rose; they were followed by anti-aircraft cannon at the strip's end. After that, the power of 2,000 horses pulled me skyward to aviation's supermortal view, until a voice in my receiver shouted, "Clear your guns!"

Now, we are spread wide—the four of us—in combat formation, so we'll have room to maneuver in attack. At the foot of those hills below, hidden in that thick jungle mat of leaves and branches, are our enemies—men of different language and ideas, but with bodies and brains quite similar to ours. We know that their glasses are now trained upon us, that their loaded batteries will antici- pate our course....

Sixteen-hundred rounds I carry, of .50-calibre ammunition, and I can spew them out at the rate of 5,000 rounds a minute. Suddenly the grace of flight is gone. I see with war-conditioned eyes—these are wicked-looking planes we fly, manned by ruthless pilots, built to kill, hoping to kill, as we approach the heavily-defended fortress of Rabaul....

—Charles A. Lindbergh, "Thoughts of a Combat Pilot," *The Saturday Evening Post*, October 2, 1954

Comdr. Ralph Milleson looks over what's left of the cockpit of his F4U-4 Corsair more than 30 years after he ditched it in Lake Washington in July 1950.

attack missions in the Pacific and in Korea, when pilots found they could spot targets from almost directly above, do wingovers, and then aim along the "hose nose," as the Corsair's long snout became known to Marine and Navy aviators.

"Although as commanding officer of VF-44 [Fighter Squadron-44] I flew the F4U-4 during the final phase of the American involvement in the Korean conflict," Vice Adm. William Houser remembers, "my first flight in a Corsair was in 1947 when I was regularly flying the small, speedy, maneuverable Grumman F8F Bearcat. The pilot of the petite Bearcat 'wore' the airplane, being seated right over the wing, just aft of the engine. In the Corsair, the pilot rode well aft, behind the engine and the fuselage fuel tank. The seat was mounted on the floor and the rudder pedals were only slightly lower than the level of the seat. Thus, a pilot's legs were almost horizontal. Sitting well aft in the airplane, I occasionally felt like a chariot rider, steering a team of horses. In fact I was steering and aiming the equivalent of some 2,000 horses at full power."

The entire airframe was so aerodynamically clean that the pilot's handbook claimed for it a dead-stick (engine out) glide ratio of thirteen-to-one, which means it would glide, unpowered, thirteen miles for each 5,000-odd feet of lost altitude.

A total of 12,571 Corsairs were built. To achieve this total, a three-company industrial combine was organized. Goodyear, the tire manufacturer, and Brewster, whose F2A Buffalo was phased out of production early in the war, also built Corsairs. The last Vought-built Corsairs, for export to France, rolled off the line in 1952, after a longer production run than that of any American fighter up to the McDonnell F-4 Phantom.

The Museum of Flight's Goodyear-built FG-1, BuAer Number 88382, was built in April 1945, and served aboard the carrier U.S.S. *Intrepid* and flew from bases in Hawaii and Saipan. Its last duty station was the Sand Point Naval Air Station in Seattle. It might have been melted down for scrap had it not been skillfully ditched in Seattle's Lake Washington on July 29, 1950 after a midair collision. Another advantage of the Corsair's gull-wing design was the ease with which it could be ditched: momentarily, at least, it became a catamaran.

In heavy overcast and unaware of each other, two divisions of naval reserve Corsairs with four aircraft apiece were flying toward Sand Point, east of the University of Washington. The leader of the division in front turned into the following division's flight path from underneath and wiped off the tail-end Corsair, flown by Ens. Sam Hayes, on the following division's leader, Comdr. Ralph Milleson. Hayes's wing and canopy clipped Milleson's propeller.

"Milleson was cool," a pilot in the lead division remembered, "but not one hundred percent cool. He revealed his excitement when he called Sand Point tower to inform them he was ditching and requested permission to ditch in the lake off the field. I don't recall whether the tower gave him permission to ditch or not."

He was cool the day the FG-1 was pulled out of the lake and brought, in remarkably good condition, to the waterfront.

"With cameras rolling," *The Seattle Times* reported, "Ralph Milleson casually strolled from the Navy-chauffeured car toward the cockpit of the aircraft he had ridden 33 years ago.... 'I just wanted to see if I left anything,' joked Milleson."

DESIGNER: REX BEISEL

Rex Beisel, father of the Corsair, is the least-known designer of a great American combat aircraft. Then again, lack of fame was the least of his problems.

Born in 1893, Beisel overcame staggering personal handicaps: the death of his father when he was a year old; a lifetime case of Parkinson's disease that worsened as he aged; deafness and color blindness; no sense of smell; and undiagnosed migraines all his life.

Devoted to his mother, who left Sweden and crossed the North American continent to California on her own, Beisel was inspired by her to seize every possible advantage. He was boarded in distant Seattle so he could attend Queen Anne High School. His stepfather, a coal mine foreman who adopted Rex when he was sixteen, got him summer jobs underground so he could afford to study engineering at the University of Washington. Tested for intelligence late in life, while an executive with the Chance Vought Corporation, Beisel was ranked in the upper quarter of one percent of the general population.

Straight out of school, he started with the agency that became the Naval Bureau of Aeronautics before the United States entered World War I, designing and stress-testing wings for Navy seaplanes. His first solo design was the first combat plane designed for operation from an aircraft carrier, the Curtiss TS, which was developed into a racer. The experience led to his design for Curtiss of the RC series of land and seaplane racers, which won the 1923 and 1925 Pulitzer races, the 1925 Schneider Cup, and set a world's speed record. Through the 1920s, Beisel, as Curtiss's chief engineer, designed mailplanes, fighters, and dive-bombers, and shared credit for the B-2 Condor bomber. The airliner version of the Condor was the American Airlines sleeper plane replaced by the DC-3.

In 1931 Beisel came to the Chance Vought Corporation, a subsidiary of United Aircraft and then the Navy's leading airframe contractor. He arrived the year Chance Vought, the firm's founder, died. It was during his time there that Vought moved to the forefront of military aircraft

Rex Beisel, designer of the Corsair, chats with ace flyer Maj. Greg "Pappy" Boyington, who gained most of his 28 victories from the cockpits of Corsairs — and was shot down in one.

design. His SB2U Vindicator was the first monoplane scout bomber, and his OS2U Kingfisher was the best scout plane of World War II. His masterpiece was, of course, the Corsair.

As an executive with Vought after 1943, Beisel supported the company's move toward developing such oddball projects as the XF5U-1 "Flying Flapjack" and the tailless F7U Cutlass (which, despite its tricky flying qualities, achieved carrier service in 1954). Beisel resigned at the age of fifty-six over United Aircraft's attempts to control its Texas Division, created when Vought moved at the Navy's request from Connecticut to Dallas in 1948. He retired to Sarasota, Florida, and died in 1972.

Climbing Like a Hungry Hawk

Frank Tallman picked out his Goodyear-built FG-1 at the naval boneyard at Litchfield, Arizona. "To an aviator and a true lover of aircraft, the sight of these proud and great Navy airplanes waiting to be picked apart like buzzards over a dead burro never ceases to make me sad. My three Corsairs"—from which he would pick one—"were at the end of a mile and a half drive between rows of Navy aircraft totalling in the thousands...."

Without too much trouble the Pratt & Whitney started with its characteristic dynamolike windup, and I taxied out following the Navy "Follow-Me" Jeep. At the takeoff point I again checked my wing fold lever by my left elbow; the tail wheel was locked, the canopy was locked (open), the open engine was OK, and all instrument readings were normal.

As I fed power I needed a lead foot (on the right rudder pedal, to compensate for the big prop's torque), and before I could catch my breath, I was airborne at about 90mph and climbing like a hungry hawk. With the gear up, prop and power back, and canopy closed, my heart decided it could beat again. With the opportunity to look around I realized what a powerhouse of an airplane this was.

Climbing on course to Blythe and settling down at 10,000 feet, I again consulted the Pilot's Aircraft Handbook. *As long as I was paying for my own fuel, I began acting like Scrooge and dropped rpm to 1,450 and began counting blades. I sailed along with 30 inches indicating, at over 200 knots.*

On these earlier Corsairs you had two foot-channels under the rudder pedals and then a free fall to the bottom of the fuselage. The hole consequently was quite large enough to lose a white-faced Hereford in, but it served another purpose. When you got tired and your legs got stiff, you could trim out the Corsair, loosen your chute, and just dangle your legs in the abyss.

Tucking my feet back on the pedals, still at cruise, I cleared myself ahead, pulled the nose above the horizon, locked on a cloud, and rolled. Because of the long nose, you can put it on a point and lock on as beautifully in a roll as you could with the long-nosed liquid-cooled jobs like the P-51 and the P-40.

The ailerons are faultless and pure delight, above a third the stick load of a P-51 at any altitude. For all its light touch there is a pleasant feeling of size and strength in the F4U that I have never felt in any fighter, except possibly a P-38....

—Frank Tallman, *Flying the Old Planes*

GOODYEAR FG-1 CORSAIR

Dimensions

Overall wingspan 40ft 11³/₄in

Overall length 33ft 8¹/₄in

Height 16ft 1in

Engine

One Pratt & Whitney R-2800-8 (W) with water
injection, 2,250hp

Weight

Empty 8,873lbs

Maximum loaded 14,000lbs

Performance

Maximum speed 395mph

Initial climb 2,890ft/min

Range on internal fuel (typical) 1,000mi

Service ceiling 37,000ft

Boeing B-47E Stratojet

The B-47's trademark takeoff was this smoky, roaring departure. Up to 30 rocket bottles attached to the rear of the fuselage gave the B-47 a big boost into the air by means of JATO (Jet Assisted Take-Off). *Facing page:* A B-47 rising on a plume of JATO exhaust symbolized the strategic ascendance of the U.S. In the early 1950s no other power was capable of delivering a thermonuclear bomb at 600mph.

More than forty years after it was designed, the B-47 Strato-jet remains the most beautiful aircraft Boeing ever created, and also the most influential. There is visible majesty in the design that shows even in those sad 1960s photos of hundreds of B-47s lined up as far as the eye can see, the onetime tip of America's nuclear deterrent waiting in the Arizona desert boneyards to be broken up and melted down.

The way the B-47 sat, nose up, looking eager to take off when it was standing still, was nothing less than arrogant. A B-47 takeoff was spectacular, especially a rocket-assisted takeoff: the arrow-shaped bomber bounded skyward at the apex of a towering triangle of smoke generated by as many as thirty 1,000-pound-thrust rocket bottles arranged in rows on each side of the rear fuselage.

It was entitled to its airs. It was the first multiengine aircraft to exceed 600 miles per hour. A peacekeeper, it was as successful as any bomber that ever went to war. The B-47's mission in the nuclear age was *not* to go to war, and it didn't. Through the 1950s, when atomic war seemed most likely, the B-47 and its thermonuclear egg were one of the cold war's main deterrents to a hot war.

Walter J. Boyne, former director of the National Air and Space Museum, who flew B-47s, wrote in a 1981 issue of *Wings* that "when the B-47 fleet was at its peak in the mid-fifties and early sixties, the United States enjoyed a measure of strategic superiority greater than any nation had enjoyed before—or since.

"In those halcyon days of the Strategic Air Command, the B-47s were virtually immune to attack. At altitude they were nearly as fast as the North American F-86s, Grumman Panthers and other fighters that vainly tried to intercept them, and it would not have been any different with MiG-15s...."

Those years of relative peace notwithstanding, the B-47's main aviation legacy is the worldwide fleet of jet airliners that have brought humanity closer together than ever before. Most of them are Boeings. All jet airliners retain elements of the B-47.

In designing the first mass-produced jet bomber, Boeing made the mold for commercial aviation. Before the

Right: Six turbojet engines gave the 90-ton bomber 36,000lbs of thrust. The only armament on early models were twin 20mm cannon in the tail. For most of its operational life, the B-47's main defenses were speed and altitude.

B-47, nobody in the United States had any idea what a big jet should look like. Certainly Boeing's engineers didn't. They went through dozens of arrangements and models, most of which look distinctly peculiar in light of the elegance of the design that emerged as the XB-47 Stratojet prototype in 1947.

As a testimonial, the Boeing Company chose to publicize the four men who contributed the most to shaping the B-47. They were Edward Wells, designer of B-17s; George Schairer, the aerodynamicist responsible for the B-47's revolutionary swept wing; George Martin, the eventual project engineer; and Robert Jewett, head of Boeing's preliminary design unit, who was involved in the initial choice between pure jet or turboprop power.

The first American jet engines were developments of the British Whittle design of 1941—volatile, very thirsty, and not very powerful. Ed Wells, busy with the B-29 project, was surprised nevertheless at how far jet power had come by September 1943, when he visited Muroc Dry Lake, California, to see the experimental Bell P-59 Airacomet, America's first jet fighter.

Boeing began work on a jet reconnaissance plane that same month. It was a project to meet a purposely vague requirement for something that didn't exist. The preliminary design showed two paired-jet nacelles under the straight wings of a slenderized B-29. In January 1944, Wells took the preliminary design to the U.S. Army Air Force's test facility at Wright Field, in Dayton, Ohio, and then to Washington, D.C. By then the Air Force had already raised its sights to the level of the medium bomber that the eventual B-47 would become. It could be either pure jet or turboprop powered.

That March, Wells and Jewett took design data on the new bomber to Dayton and Washington. No technical requirement for the jet bomber yet existed, although the Air Force was now leaning toward the jet engine, rather than the turboprop, and was unofficially looking for a minimum speed of 400mph. Both power options had their attractions: the Soviets were resolving the same question in favor of the turboprop, for increased range.

All of which led to Schairer's decisive argument that, for the Air Force's preferred pure jet to be efficient, the aircraft had to fly at much more than 400mph. At that speed, he said, "you're just pushing air and burning up your fuel. You won't get any range."

During April the Air Force issued a request for proposals that stipulated 500mph, a ceiling of 40,000 feet, and a tactical radius of 1,000 miles. Things were moving fast. Three other companies with bomber backgrounds—North American, Convair, and Martin—were invited to submit proposals for the new jet bomber.

The resulting series of tests involved trying and rejecting each of three configurations before starting on detailed design of the fourth. Some feature of each failure appeared on the final Boeing Model 450-1-1, designated B-47 by the Air Force. This time-consuming design process was possible only because Wells was willing to risk not being first in order to be best. It is interesting to note that the other three contenders were variations on Boeing's first, and already rejected, scheme.

The most difficult question, in the end, was where to install the engines. For reasons of wing efficiency, it would have been nice to keep them off the wing. The American jet fighters that had appeared so far buried them within the fuselage, allowing undisturbed airflow over the wing and control surfaces.

It was with that principle in mind that the first configuration, Boeing's Model 424, the slenderized B-29 with its podded pairs of jets slung from the wings, was dropped in favor of a layout with the six engines specified by the Air Force buried high in the fuselage shoulder, over the wings, fed from cheek intakes on each side of the cockpit. They made for a rather portly fuselage. That was the scheme—Boeing's Model 432, submitted to the Air Force in December 1944, along with the proposals from Convair, Martin, and North American.

"Model 432 was an almost classical expression of the 1944 dilemma facing aero-engineers," Walter Boyne wrote in his 1981 study of the B-47's development. "The L/D (Lift to Drag) ratio of straight wings fell off drastically at Mach

"At altitude, in the early days, you had an exclusive. You were the only ones there. If you saw a contrail, it had to be another B-47."

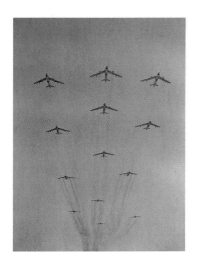

Thirty-five-degree "arrowhead" swept-wing design was derived from German wartime test data, which verified that such wings could improve flights at speeds approaching the speed of sound.

.6"—a speed that decreases with altitude, but is around 400mph at sea level—"because of the vastly increased drag due to Mach effect," the shock wave generated by an aerodynamic body moving though the air at those speeds.

"On the other hand," Boyne continues, echoing Schairer's thoughts of 1944, "at speeds below Mach .6, jet engines were only two-thirds as efficient as contemporary reciprocating engines."

Once efficient speeds for jets were reached, engineers such as Schairer were expecting problems with flight surfaces to set in. Since 1935, aerodynamicists had been theorizing that swept-back wings might fall within the shock cone created by the nose of an aircraft flying faster than the speed of sound, and thus create less drag. The first to propose such a possibility was Adolf Busemann, who had been fascinated by the bow wakes of ships in the port of his childhood home, the port city of Lübeck, Germany. His application of that insight to aircraft at a 1935 conference in Rome led him to advocate what he called "arrow wings." He was ridiculed.

An American, the self-taught aero-engineer Robert T. Jones of the National Advisory Committee for Aeronautics (NACA), was on the same track. His airflow theory, called "subsonic sweep," was confirmed after considerable controversy by supersonic wind-tunnel tests at NACA's Langley laboratory, just as World War II was ending.

While the ungainly Model 432 approach was being tested in Seattle during the spring of 1945, Germany collapsed. George Schairer was appointed to the Scientific Advisory Board of the Army Air Force, chaired by the Hungarian-born Cal Tech aerodynamicist Theodor von Kármán. The board was formed to learn as much as possible from the results of the Luftwaffe's high-speed aerodynamic research, then the best in the world.

Before he left for Germany, Schairer found himself talking to a Chinese professor, Hsu Shen Tsien, at the Pentagon, who brought up Jones's notion about "subsonic sweep." The two did calculations all night during the flight to Paris. Neither could disprove the theory.

The morning Germany surrendered, Schairer and his colleagues were casing Luftwaffe chief Hermann Göring's top-secret Aeronautical Research Institute at Braunschweig, in northern Germany. It was impressive: fifty-six buildings, some camouflaged as farmhouses, some underground, isolated from one another to preserve secrecy, complete with a concealed airfield. A thousand people had worked there.

In his memoir, *The Wind and Beyond*, Kármán recalls that "we walked into one room of the aerodynamics building and there on a desk was a model of a plane that we had not seen before. It had sweptback wings, like the head of an arrow. George Schairer was quite excited when he saw that model, and so was I. It represented the new type of ultrafast plane of the future...."

"The Germans, I knew, were under orders to destroy all documents of a certain classification on receipt of a code word, and we had indeed seen several piles of ashes indicating the orders were carried out. But I felt sure the Germans had not had the time to destroy or remove everything, and that quite likely as with all bureaucratic organizations there were duplicate copies. But where could the plans be hidden? There were literally thousands of hiding places. I asked the German director of Braunschweig, but he said out of patriotism, or perhaps fear of the Germans' return, that he didn't know. I wasn't convinced.

"I had with me a sergeant assigned by Intelligence. Frank Tchitcherine was of Russian origin.... As we were walking to our automobile with the director, I said in English, which I knew the director understood, 'Listen, Tchitcherine, we are through here. I think now it is time to notify Russian intelligence to take over.'

"Russian intelligence was nowhere in the vicinity. But I knew the Germans were terrified of the Russians.... The next day the director called in Tchitcherine and took him to a dry well. He looked inside. It was full of documents."

Schairer quickly saw the names of men he knew had studied under Kármán. He recognized formulas he'd been working out with Hsu Shen Tsien. It all looked solid to Schairer.

The next day Kármán called Busemann.

"Don't you remember?" Busemann asked—Rome, 1935?

Now Kármán remembered. So did Schairer. "You just don't see a thing until you want to see it," Schairer told his Boeing colleague George Martin, in Europe with another group. "Then you find the answer you need has been there all the time."

Schairer wrote a personal letter home to his replace-

The future of military and commercial aviation stood on the tarmac at Boeing Field in December 1947 The new XB-47 set the pattern for most large commercial and military aircraft for the remainder of the century.

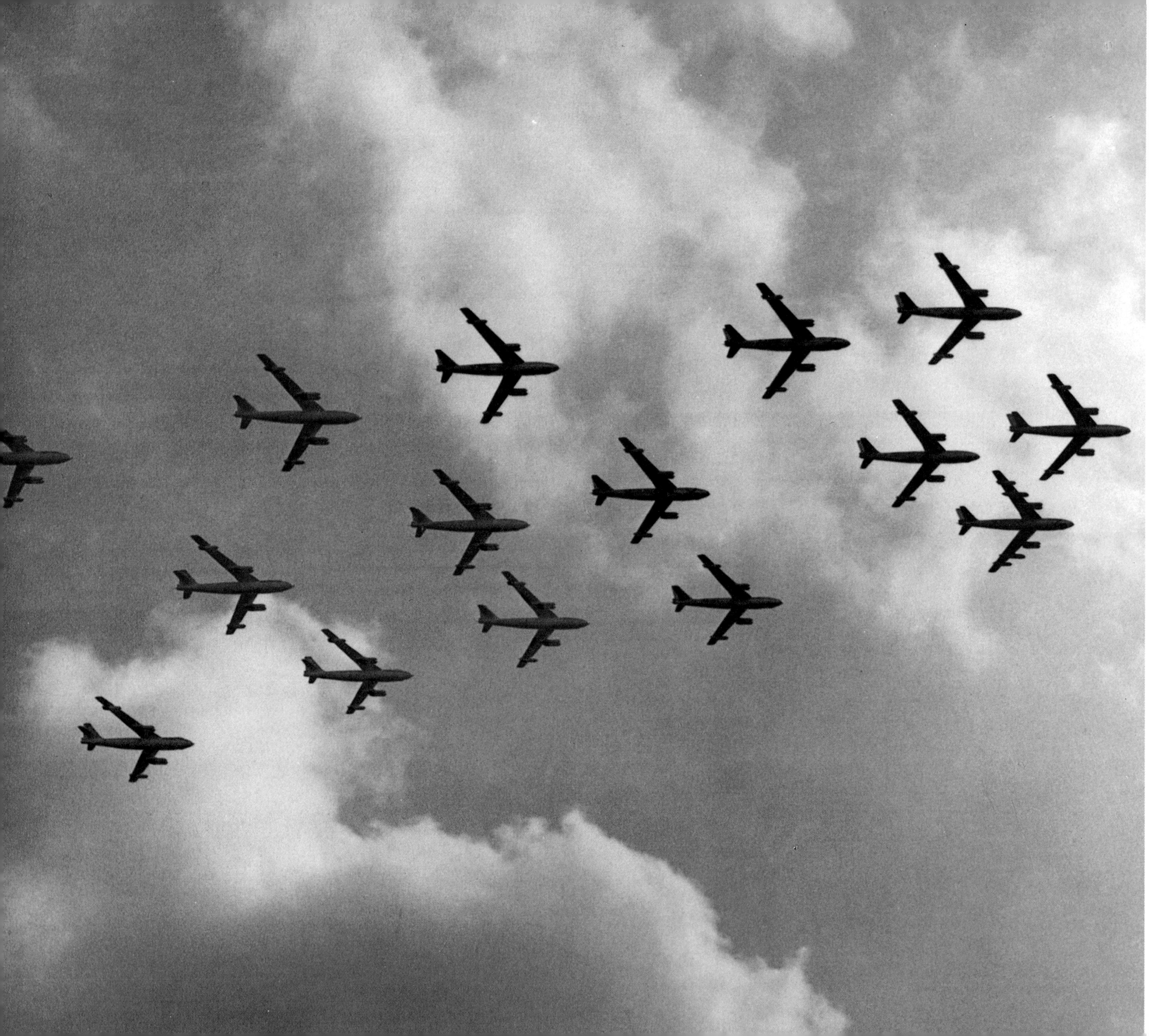

ment, Ben Cohn, illustrating it with a drawing of the swept wings he was suggesting for the new bomber.

This was the third configuration, Model 448: forty-five-degree swept wings on a fuselage with four engines still buried behind the cockpit, fed by a "fishmouth" air inlet in the nose, and two more engines with their own inlets at the rear. On September 13, 1945, Boeing formally proposed swept wings to Wright Field.

The problem with these two fuselage-engine layouts was how to protect the rear of the airframe from the heat of the jet blast. Another problem was where to put all the fuel, which could be stored neither in the wings, because of their thinness, nor in the fuselage near the engines. Operationally, of course, four engines bunched together over the wings would be vulnerable to a single burst of fire from fighters. By now North American, Martin, and Convair had contracts to build prototype jet bombers. The pressure was on Boeing.

After getting the thumbs-down from the staff at Wright Field over survivability of the engines, Wells and Jewett repaired to their hotel room in Dayton and tried to think of something else to do with the powerplants. Wells remembered some data Schairer had brought back from Germany about jet engines suspended on struts.

Cohn gave it a try in the wind tunnel. Suspending the engines from the wings on pylons was the inspiration that made the B-47 great. Everything else now fell into place. It left much of the airflow over and under the wings undisturbed. If the engines were set far enough ahead of the wings, their drag turned out to be no greater than if they were buried in the body. The fuselage was now slimmer. Four of the six engines, paired in pods inboard on the wing, and single engines out at the tips, distributed the weight better, enabling the airframe to be lightened. That added range.

Boeing's conceptual sketch of the fourth scheme, Model 450-1-1, showing off the podded engines from ahead and slightly below, became the classic B-47 pose. The only important change from concept to prototype was to add sixteen feet to the wingspan and drop the wingtip engines down, on their own pods. That added ceiling and, consequently, range. And it looked even better. "The design that's most right is also the most beautiful," Wells said.

The Only Ones There

The B-47 brought joy to the hearts of bomber pilots. After years of listening to garrulous fighter pilots spieling endlessly about their responsive mounts, of enduring their witless barroom jibes about aerial truck drivers... we bomber pilots suddenly had in the B-47 a plane that was almost fighter-like in its flying qualities....

The sleek lines of the airplane gave one a first impression of speed and liveliness that familiarity did not dim. The fighter-like cockpit with its blown canopy and tandem seating added to this feeling. But most important was the fact that the B-47 was responsive in all flight regimes. At very heavy weights, on hot days, and at high altitudes, it was sluggish on takeoff and runways did tend to seem very short....

But even under these conditions, once airborne, the B-47 assumed almost regal characteristics. Its speed was exhilarating; for pilots brought up on four flailing piston engines, the climb speed of the B-47, starting at 310 knots indicated airspeed, was heady....

The visibility from the B-47's cockpit was superb; and at altitude, in the early days, you had an exclusive. You were the only ones there. If you saw a contrail, it had to be another B-47.

—Walter Boyne (B-47 pilot), "Bomber 47," *Wings*, August 1981

Without the sophisticated flap systems of more recent Boeing swept-wing jets, the B-47 required braking parachutes. Late models, like this B-47E, used two chutes — a small one to achieve low approach speed while retaining enough power for an emergency go-around, and a large one to assist braking.

At the wooden mock-up stage, in April 1946, the air staff from Wright had only one quibble: the Rube Goldberg tricycle landing gear sprouting from various doors under the fuselage. A bicycle arrangement had been designed and tested for Martin's jet bomber entry (which did not achieve production), and that was the final touch for the B-47. With short wheel-bogies at the bottom of the fuselage ahead of the wing and behind it, augmented by small outrigger wheels positioned between the engines in the inboard pods, the B-47 now had its characteristic regal air on the ground.

Its appearance of being in flight while standing still was not entirely an illusion. The nose-high stance allowed the B-47 to be literally taxied off the ground without being rotated upward. Test pilot Bob Robbins, aboard with Scott Osler for the first flight of the XB-47, on December 17, 1947, had no idea he was off the ground when the jet cleared the runway shortly after 2:02 p.m. He was reaching for the rocket-assist switch when the Boeing Field tower told him he was airborne. It was that smooth.

Though it was a peacetime warplane, the Museum of Flight's B-47 Stratojet enjoyed a career that, toward its end, was often fraught with danger. It accumulated more than 6,000 flying hours before being retired to Boeing Field in October 1969. It was one of the last handful of operational B-47s.

Serial number 51-7066, built in 1951, was the second B-47E-75-BW off the line. The E model was the definitive B-47, with ejection seats and water-injected engines for brief surges of additional power. The number 75 refers to the particular production block, which comprised nineteen aircraft, and BW signifies the Boeing Wichita plant, where the majority of B-47s were produced. (Production blocks, a concept pioneered during World War II, result from small changes incorporated in military aircraft on the production line. All aircraft in a block are alike in detail.)

The B-47 was regarded as such an advance in bomber technology that it was produced under a high-priority program reminiscent of wartime that included Lockheed and Douglas. A total of 2,041 were built.

Refinished today in its 1956–63 markings of the 384th Bombardment Wing, based at Little Rock, the Museum of Flight's B-47 carried the Strategic Air Command colors to England in 1958 and 1963 during SAC's "Reflex Action" alerts.

In November 1963 this aircraft was converted by Lockheed-Georgia into one of thirty-four WB-47E (W for weather) flying weather laboratories that transmitted data to ground stations on behalf of the Air Weather Service (AWS) of the U.S. Air Force. The AWS B-47s also monitored weather conditions at splashdown sites during the early manned-spacecraft programs. Although B-47s were structurally prohibited from flying directly into hurricanes and typhoons, they often monitored such storms, capping their careers with what turned out to be the most dangerous duties of their peacetime operational lives. This B-47 was flown direct to Boeing Field from its last posting, in Hawaii.

BOEING B-47E STRATOJET

Dimensions

Overall wingspan 116ft

Overall length 109ft 10in

Height 27ft 11in

Engines

Six General Electric J47-GE-25 axial-flow turbojets
rated at 5,970lbs static thrust each, 7,200lbs static thrust with
water injection

Weight

Empty 78,200lbs

Loaded (10,000lb bombload) 206,700lbs

Performance

Maximum speed . . . . 606mph at 16,300ft

Cruising speed . . . . Mach .75–.82

Service altitude 32,000–38,000ft

(differences due to fuel burnoff during mission)

Crew 3

Hiller YH-32 Hornet Helicopter

Stanley Hiller Jr. was one of those pioneers of vertical flight who foresaw a helicopter in every garage. Instead of walking, pedestrians would fly their own minicopters. When a February 1951 *Popular Mechanics* cover illustration showed a suburbanite backing a bright yellow helicopter into his garage while his neighbor flew overhead in a red one, the flying machines looked surprisingly like the Hiller Hornet, which had been announced that same year.

The late 1940s and early 1950s were a fertile period for the exploration of Vertical Takeoff and Landing (VTOL) concepts of all kinds. Turboprop fighters that sat on their tails and took off like rockets, "convertiplanes" that hovered like helicopters and used conventional propellers for horizontal flight, and various tilt-wing and tilt-rotor aircraft in which the rotors worked both as propellers and as lift devices were being built and tested. Stanley Hiller, designer of the YH-32 Hornet, an experimental helicopter powered by rotor-tip ramjets, was one of the most prolific innovators of that era.

Hiller became interested in helicopters in 1941, at the age of sixteen, after seeing pictures and films of Igor Sikorsky's first helicopter flights. When he decided to build his own helicopters, his first goal was to eliminate the tail rotor, which he felt robbed the lifting rotors of too much power that could otherwise contribute to direct lift. This may sound precocious for a sixteen-year-old, but Stanley Hiller was no ordinary teenager.

Six years before, he had constructed a toy automobile that he reportedly drove through the streets of Berkeley. At twelve he developed the Hiller Comet, a 19-inch model racing car that, according to a contemporary account, could do 107 miles per hour, guided by a cable around a circular course. Backed by his shipping-executive father and namesake, he formed Hiller Industries, which mass-produced these sophisticated models with aluminum bodies formed by a technique young Hiller invented for die-casting non-ferrous metals. This technique was used during World War II to manufacture aircraft parts such as window frames for the C-47, the military version of the DC-3. The Navy requested a draft deferment for Hiller, to enable him to continue his experimental work.

He formed the Hiller Aircraft Corporation in 1942 and developed the XH-44 Hiller-Copter, a double-rotor craft that was his first attempt to solve the basic problem of helicopters: the torque, or twisting force generated by the engine, that makes helicopters want to spin in the direction opposite that of the whirling rotors. Hiller patented his system of coaxial double rotors that turn on a common shaft in opposite directions, canceling out each other's torque. In its public appearances, the machine's rotor drive and control mechanism was covered by canvas gloves to keep its design secret. Six men designed and built the Hiller-Copter, including Hiller and Harold Sigler, who engineered and sketched out the teenager's ideas, making design contributions of his own.

Aside from being the first workable coaxial helicopter, the XH-44 was the first helicopter to fly west of the Mississippi and the first to use rigid, all-metal rotors, a feature unmatched by other manufacturers for more than a decade.

Yet another first: The XH-44 was the first truly stable helicopter—so stable that Hiller often demonstrated it with both of his hands extended from the cockpit during flight. His work attracted financial support from the shipbuilder Henry J. Kaiser, who made Hiller's small group the Hiller-Copter Division of the Kaiser Cargo Company. The business arrangement ended in 1945 when Kaiser embarked upon his ill-fated "Henry J" carmaking venture. That year, Hiller formed United Helicopters Inc., to continue his work toward developing a simplified, easy-to-fly, low-cost rotary-wing aircraft.

"Hiller is mature beyond his years," wrote the author of a *Flying* magazine profile of the nineteen-year-old inventor-entrepreneur that appeared six months after the first untethered flight of the XH-44 at the University of California Stadium, Berkeley, on May 14, 1944. "He exhibits no signs of self-consciousness as he sits in his panelled office, responds to inter-communication system calls, or handles a Washington long-distance call.

"He is six feet tall, thin, and energetic. He speaks with reserve until the subject of flying is brought up. Then he becomes enthusiastic...."

In 1946 he crashed in his latest XH-44 model. He then showed his flexibility by adopting the more conventional tail-rotor approach to controlling torque. The result was a milestone of helicopter design, the three-seat Hiller 360. It first flew under the company designation UH-12 (UH for United Helicopters) and was certified by the Civil Aeronautics Authority (CAA) in 1948. Over the next two years, Hiller sold more helicopters for commercial use than all other manufacturers combined: a total of eighty-two.

During the early fifties the 360 achieved a measure of fame in Vietnam, where a French Army captain, Valérie André, won the Croix de Guerre for flying solo medical evacuation missions—the first routine airlifts of wounded soldiers in history. Already an experienced parachutist and fixed-wing pilot, André joined the French army straight out of medical school, served a year in what was then French Indochina, was trained to fly helicopters, and returned to the war in 1950. Flying many of her sorties under fire, she eventually rescued 165 wounded soldiers.

War in Korea increased Hiller's work force from 100 to 700, and the company eventually delivered more than 2,000 of the 360/UH-12 series over a production life of twenty years. Models included the Navy's HTE-1 and -2, the Army H-23 (later named Raven), and hundreds more sold to the air arms of a dozen countries. The 360/UH-12 series was intensively developed over its long life: the first thousand-hours-between-overhauls helicopter was the Army's H-23D of 1957. The 12E, introduced in 1958, was a much-improved development of the 360 and was widely regarded as the finest piston-engine helicopter ever built. Many were still in service as Army trainers during the mid-seventies.

(The Museum of Flight also exhibits a perfectly restored example of the Hiller 12E, one of the two crop-dusting helicopters with which Oregon-based Evergreen International Aviation was founded in 1960.)

Hiller's adoption of the most widely accepted powertrain formula for helicopters didn't stop him and his engineers from continuing to explore a variety of approaches to the VTOL problem. Hiller Helicopters, as he had renamed his company to avoid confusion with the helicopter division of United Aircraft, was working during the early fifties on the Flying Platform, a ducted-fan aircraft controlled by the pilot's body inclination. Another approach was the Navy–Marine Corps XROE-1 Rotorcycle of 1957, a one-man helicopter which could be collapsed into a parachute-droppable package and then quickly assembled with quick-release pins. Seven were built for the Navy and five more for commercial use. Late in the decade, the Hiller company was also at work on a tilt-wing "propelloplane," the X-18, whose wings (and the engines mounted on them) tilted up for takeoff or landing and rotated to horizontal for conventional flight. This project led to a transport-size VTOL prototype aircraft, the four-engine XC-142A, a joint venture among Ling-Temco-Vought, Hiller, and the Ryan Aircraft Corporation.

In 1951, Hiller unveiled another remarkable design, the rotor-tip ramjet-powered HJ-1 Hornet. This could have been the simplified, cheap, easy-to-fly helicopter he had been aiming for all along. At 7 feet tall, with a 23-foot rotor, it would fit in some garages, and at the announced price of less

than $5,000 it was competitive at the time with a sports car. Hiller fully intended the Hornet to be the Volkswagen of helicopters.

Those plans were shelved with the outbreak of hostilities in Korea. Nevertheless, a test batch of twelve of a slightly larger (7ft 8in) prototype with a tail rotor, the YH-32, was ordered by the Army in 1952 and delivered in 1956. A single Navy prototype was built but not accepted.

The Museum of Flight's military YH-32 Hornet was found in a garage — and in bad enough shape for the finder to wonder what it was. It was bought by Stanley Hiller, who had it restored and donated it to the Museum.

The Hiller company's idea was to eliminate most of the normal helicopter's weight by using rotor-tip powerplants "to eliminate antitorque requirements, complex engine installations, and large power transmission systems," as project engineer Harvey Holm explained at a helicopter design seminar in Los Angeles in 1953.

As Stanley Hiller explained to his biographer, former Museum of Flight curator Jay Spenser, the YH-32 Hornet was a proof-of-concept vehicle, intended to demonstrate the feasibility of rotor-tip power for an eventual giant "flying crane." Building the dozen Army test craft and using them in field conditions would prove the soundness of the rotor-tip power concept. In the giant flying crane, powertrain weight savings would translate directly into increased payload. The U.S. armed forces were eager to have such machines, and the concept appeared sound. Howard Hughes, no stranger to outsized aircraft concepts, built a flying test bed, the XH-17, with a main rotor diameter of 130ft, powered by compressed air carried along the rotors to tip nozzles from two platform-mounted jet engines. It flew in 1952, and had it gone into production, it would have been the first helicopter to carry its own weight in useful load: a maximum loaded weight of 105,000 pounds. The ramjets Hiller was developing for the YH-32 would have been more efficient at the high speeds reached by the tips of such long rotors.

For these rotor-tip powerplants Hiller developed the first ramjet engines ever certified by the CAA — in fact, the first American-designed and -built jet engines of any kind to be so endorsed. Ramjets have no moving parts and, because of their simplicity, can be very small. They are fed with air by their forward motion through it. A flameholder at the front with a fuel nozzle and ignition line ignites the fuel-air mixture. A combustion chamber from which the hot exhaust gases emerge completes the engine.

At very high speeds ramjets become efficient, and since rotor-tip speeds can approach the speed of sound, these small engines seemed better than anything then available for such use. Hiller had been working to develop the ramjet through the late 1940s and had solved the problems involved in making engine parts from a heat-resistant but hard-to-form nickel alloy, Inconel X. The company had evolved a ramjet that was the size of a medium-sized watermelon, weighed 12.7lbs, developed 40lbs static thrust apiece (or 45 equivalent horsepower), and could be removed in minutes with a screwdriver, "even though," as Holm wrote, "the fuel flow rates then quoted for sub-sonic ramjets were little short of shocking."

The result was a paragon of simplicity and functional design. During two years of company testing it was discovered that the more-or-less-conventional rudder used on the flying test stand (Hiller Model XHJ-1) offered less positive yaw control than a small tail rotor, especially in crosswinds and at low rotor speeds during landing. The question of using tail rotors was decided by the military requirement for controlled lateral movement, so the military Hornets were designed with them after all.

It took five minutes to accelerate the rotors to 50rpm by means of a small gasoline engine, since the ramjet cannot develop thrust while standing still. This might have proven troublesome in a battlefield environment but presumably would have allowed a morning commuter time for one last cup of coffee.

The fuel system, Holm explained to his professional colleagues in the summer of 1953, got tricky where the fuel had to be transferred to the whirling rotor blades on its way to the thirsty ramjets. A rotary seal at the bottom of the rotor installation and a "splitter tee" at the rotor head got the fuel on its way out along the blades, where centrifugal force took over. Unfortunately, this meant the fuel pressure varied according to rpm, from the 25–40 pounds per square inch developed by the fuel pump to as much as 2,500psi at maximum speed. This made quick acceleration or deceleration impossible because of the amount of fuel in the lines at any given time and the high pressures the system built up. And pilots like nothing more than immediate response when they operate the throttle.

Considering how advanced the power concept for the Hiller Hornet was, it seems almost unbelievable that the simple fiberglass tail boom was the most troublesome aspect of the manufacturing program. But fiberglass as a structural material was new in the early fifties. After trying various shapes, different chemical impregnation methods, and lay-up molding processes, by 1953 Hiller felt they had the problem licked.

In the end, the Hiller Hornet concept was limited by two obvious factors. First, the problem of "shocking" fuel use in ramjets worked against the idea of a lightweight helicopter. As it was, the military test Hornets carried fifty gallons of fuel, good for twenty minutes aloft; they would have needed to carry huge fuel tanks to have any kind of useful range. Second, of course, they were colossally noisy.

Though the Hiller company became what it was because of the Model 360 and Korean War production, it was that same war that wrote finis to Hiller's dream of a helicopter for everyman. Not every infantryman proved a good pilot. Good pilots thought the flying machines would become "backyard death-traps in the hands of amateur aviators." Not to mention the air traffic control nightmare.

These delightfully cartoony, egg-shaped helicopters turned out to be no more than a sidelight in America's assumption of leadership in helicopter technology after World War II. The powerplant and power-transmission problems with helicopters have never been solved, but they have been substantially mitigated by the development of turbo-shaft engines that offer power-to-weight ratios three times better than those of the piston engines that powered the first Sikorsky models. Since the Hiller Hornet appeared, power-plant technology has basically overshadowed the drawbacks of the conventional helicopter.

Dimensions

Rotor blade diameter 23ft

Height (top of rotor) 7ft 8in

Engines

Two Hiller-designed 8RJ2B ramjets, 11lbs each, developing 40lbs static thrust, equal to 45hp

Weight

Empty 544lbs

Loaded 1,080lbs

Performance

Maximum speed 80mph

Normal cruise 69mph

Rate of climb 700ft/min

Service ceiling 6,900ft

Range (two passengers) 28mi

Douglas A-4F Skyhawk II

Designed as a nuclear bomber, the A-4 extended its career by performing as an agile fighter and later becoming a worldwide entertainer.

Designed in 1952 as a light bomber for delivering nuclear weapons with pinpoint accuracy from aircraft carriers, the A-4 Skyhawk became capable over its long service life of carrying half its own weight in fuel and conventional explosives—remarkable enough in itself. What makes the Skyhawk really stand out, though, is that this bantam weightlifter turned out to be quicker and more agile than most of the pure fighters of its era.

The Museum of Flight's A-4, as its gleaming navy blue finish and polished silver intakes and wing leading edges indicate, performed aerobatics for thirteen years with the U.S. Navy's aerial demonstration team, the Blue Angels. For an aircraft designed as a bomber to extend its already lengthy active career by doing aerial gymnastics may be unprecedented in the history of military flight.

No wonder. The A-4 was the masterpiece of one of America's foremost aircraft designers, Ed Heinemann, whose career lasted from the phaseout of biplanes to the age of dash speeds that exceed Mach 2.

Because of the success of American combat aircraft designers during World War II in making their planes more capable by adding size, weight, and power, the first generation of jet-powered American combat aircraft had become expensive and difficult to maintain without offering the single quality a military pilot values the most: speed.

Heinemann was the first combat aircraft engineer to design an attack plane that added to its capabilities by subtracting weight. It required original thinking to surmise that one might add to the range of an aircraft by subtracting fuel—and therefore weight—rather than adding it (and, of course, the tanks necessary to carry it).

That same weight-saving principle had been applied ruthlessly to every other aspect of the design of a fighter project Heinemann's team was working on in 1951. This was the F4D Skyray, which would become, in October 1953, the first carrier-borne fighter to hold the world's absolute speed record. So the Navy Bureau of Aeronautics (BuAer) asked Heinemann to apply his design credo, "Simplicate and add lightness," to an attack plane, or light bomber.

The result was an attack plane, the A-4 Skyhawk, with the agility, lightness, and aerobatic capabilities of a fighter. Fighter planes had been converted to attack planes before. But never before had an attack-plane designer started by designing in the aerobatic qualities expected in a fighter plane.

During the early 1950s, both Heinemann and his counterpart at Lockheed, Clarence "Kelly" Johnson, were concerned about the increasing complexity and weight of American military aircraft. It came as a shock to American pilots in Korea to find themselves flying expensive and sophisticated aircraft that lacked the speed and climbing ability of their opponents' relatively crude MiG-15s.

Below: Surrounded on three sides by aluminum, the Number 4 Blue Angel, flying the slot position, requires perfect touch. *Above*: Lt. Pat Walsh's Blue Angel A-4. *Facing page*: A-4s lined up aboard USS *Bon Homme Richard* in March 1968, during the all-out effort to support the Marines at Khe Sanh, Vietnam.

Johnson took that message and turned it into the F-104 Starfighter, the "Missile with a Man in It," which broke every record for speed and altitude performance for fighter planes in 1958. But the Starfighter's safety was always in question because of its minimal wings, which made it tricky to handle both in the air and on the ground. It lasted less than ten years in the U.S. Air Force's frontline inventory, and its safety record became a scandal with West Germany's peacetime Luftwaffe.

Heinemann took the same message and turned it into the Skyhawk, which not only lasted until the late 1960s in Navy fleet service and until the mid-seventies with the

The Darn Thing Will Almost Scare You

This airplane is much more responsive than any other A-4 that I've ever driven. I've flown the A-4 in combat and I flew the A-7 for six years prior to coming here and I've also flown the F-4 and none of them compare with this airplane as far as responsiveness is concerned. It caged my eyeballs when I jammed the power on the first time. I didn't get any check-out in this airplane at all. I just came down here and they put me in the thing and away I went. Three days later, I was in the diamond going up and down the beach out there. Even now, this airplane brings a grin to my face.

I'll tell you, when we're in the diamond and do the high-performance takeoff, and all I get to look at is a little screw under the leading edge of the Boss' wing, you really don't get an appreciation for the airplane. It's when you're out by yourself that the darn thing will almost scare you because it's got so much power. On a high-performance takeoff, it'll go almost straight up. We've never briefed more than 94 percent power ever, and, on a cool day, we're at 92 percent. It's really got more power than we need.

—Lt. Comdr. Don Simmons (slot, Blue Angels), 1978, quoted in *Air Classics Quarterly Review*, Spring 1979

Marines, it was also used well into the 1980s to simulate the lethal maneuverability of such opponents as the Soviet MiG-21 at the Navy's "Top Gun" fighter-pilot school. Because of its comparative low cost, simplicity of maintenance, and fine subsonic performance, the Skyhawk remains in the inventory of many Third World countries and may therefore have been involved in more conflicts since it was introduced in 1955 than any other Western combat plane.

But the A-4's most remarkable assignment was as the mount for the Blue Angels. The Museum of Flight A-4 is a veteran of hundreds of Blue Angel performances. For an attack plane to do a job normally assigned to small, lightly loaded trainer aircraft or fighters shows how well the Skyhawk could be adapted to tasks Heinemann never envisioned when he drew its rakish lines.

The Navy's 1951 requirement was for a tactical aircraft that could carry a 2,000-pound bomb but weigh no more than 30,000lbs. "Mr. Attack Aviation," as Heinemann was by then known to the Navy, proposed a design at half that weight. It left the BuAer officials, who had learned to expect radical ideas from him, unsure that he could pull it off this time—even though he had prepared them for the surprise.

In November 1951, Heinemann presented BuAer with his personal thoughts on saving weight and complexity in a carrier-borne fighter jet. The essence was that every pound saved at the design stage could be multiplied by a basic growth factor over the operational life of the aircraft. Military aircraft become heavier as new equipment and more powerful engines become available. In this case, Heinemann calculated the eventual saving in gross weight to be a factor of ten; in other words, save a pound now, lose ten later. By paring deadweight to an incredible 6,000lbs, and using one of the new jet engine designs with 6,000lbs or more thrust, Heinemann thought he could achieve an unprecedented one-to-one thrust ratio and, consequently, supersonic performance. (Most fighter jets of the time were operating with thrust under forty percent of their weight, and no operational fighter had exceeded the speed of sound.) BuAer was so impressed that one officer, listening from the front row, remarked, "We just canceled our requirement for interceptors."

Soon after, Douglas Aircraft, Heinemann's company, offered a proposal that would be 100 knots faster than the Navy attack requirement, carry its load 100 miles farther, and do so at *less than half* the specified weight. "I do not believe such a thing had ever happened before and I know it has not happened since," the English aviation journalist Bill Gunston, an admirer of American warplane development during the 1950s, wrote in 1974.

It took Heinemann fourteen days "and most of fourteen nights," Gunston tells us, to create the outline of the Skyhawk. His idea was to "take the best engine I could get, stick a wing underneath and put a saddle for the jockey on top—and leave out the rest."

Despite its skepticism, the Navy asked Heinemann to double the bombload and add 100 miles to the combat radius.

ENGINEER: ED HEINEMANN

"The engineering team at Douglas Aircraft El Segundo Division, which I headed from the late 1930s into the early 1960s, produced some pretty good airplanes," Ed Heinemann writes in *Aircraft Design*, the book that distills everything he learned into a 130-page volume. "Because of the success these planes enjoyed, it is fair to say we must have been doing something right."

Gustave Henry Edward Heinemann—"quite a handle," he acknowledges in his autobiography, "but one chosen out of respect for certain relatives"—was born on March 14, 1908, in Saginaw, Michigan. In 1915 his family moved to California, where he saw the pioneer barnstormer Lincoln Beachey fly his Curtiss Pusher at the Panama-Pacific International Exposition. There, too, he had his first glimpse of the company he helped make great when he witnessed a test flight of the Douglas Cloudster. Heinemann grew into a tall, thin man whose aircraft designs were as spare and hard-working as he was.

Heinemann learned from one of the visionaries of American aviation, John K. Northrop, with whom he worked on the A-17, a forerunner of his own SBD Dauntless dive-bomber. In accepting praise for the Dauntless, victor in the Battle of Midway, Heinemann shows characteristic ambivalence about his life's work: "The Dauntless turned out to be the right plane at the right place for the right war, if there is such an ignominious thing as the right war."

His next notable design was the twin-engine A-20 Havoc, used on every front during World War II. Another wartime triumph for Heinemann and his team was the A-26 Invader, which was still in widespread use during the Korean conflict.

As impressive as the Skyhawk's engineering was, the A-4 was something of an encore for Heinemann, who had already astounded the officers at the Navy Bureau of Aeronautics with his appetite for exceeding their most ambitious requirements.

Over twelve hours one night in June 1944, Heinemann and a few colleagues determined the basic layout, specifications, and performance of what became the AD-1 Skyraider, the Skyhawk's piston-engined ancestor and eventual combat partner in Vietnam. The AD-1 became known as "the flying dumptruck" because of its ability to carry twice its weight in bombs and external fuel tanks.

Heinemann's overnight cram session came about because the Navy had its doubts about his proposed successor to the Dauntless, a prewar design that was by then obsolete. At a meeting in Washington that month, Heinemann could see that his new proposal was getting nowhere. He asked for a month to revise it.

The future of Douglas El Segundo, with no further military contracts, was on the line. But the Navy didn't have a month to spare. The Normandy landings were barely under way. The assistant chief of BuAer, Rear Adm. Laurence B. Richardson, gave Heinemann until "oh-nine-hundred tomorrow." He did it: by noon the next day Heinemann knew he had won nine months for a complete redesign and construction of a prototype.

By November 1944, Heinemann, a notable pep-talker, was able to tell the workers at El Segundo that the new plane would be underweight. "If 1,000 pounds are saved," the bulletin said, the design that would become the Skyraider "will be able to double its normal bombload and still meet specified performance."

The Skyraider prototype flew two weeks ahead of schedule, barely nine months later, on March 18, 1945. Although it had come too late for World War II, it served in Korea, was retired, and then was brought into service again for Vietnam, more than twenty years after it first flew—setting a standard of longevity in a combat aircraft beaten only by "Heinemann's Hot Rod," the Skyhawk.

Guaranteed satisfaction: The double-delta wing and tail layout of the Skyhawk made any snapshot of the Blue Angels team in action a work of art. *Below*: Bingo! Mirror-image precision, canopy to canopy on the deck.

ment, allowing it a long operational life. The Skyhawk's most outstanding achievement was its being in continuous production for no fewer than twenty-six years, believed to be a record manufacturing run for an American combat plane. During that time 2,960 Skyhawks were produced, many of them upgraded more than once during their lifetimes and exported to any of eight overseas operators.

In 1974, several years after Skyhawks were replaced as frontline combat aircraft with the fleet, special A-4 Skyhawk IIs were issued to the Blue Angels to replace their big, twin-engined F-4 Phantoms. Aerial demonstration teams like to perform their routines within a three-mile radius of their audiences. With the Phantom that couldn't be done; it couldn't turn fast enough. By contrast, with the Skyhawk, the Blue Angels had to be careful not to exceed their narrator's ability to describe what they were doing overhead.

The Museum of Flight Skyhawk, BuAer 154180 and the tenth A-4F built, carries the number 4 on its tail, emblematic of the slot position, directly behind and below the leader's aircraft in the Blue Angel diamond formation. Flying slot requires perfect touch. Lt. Pat Walsh, this plane's final Blue Angel pilot, flew surrounded on three sides by aluminum when the soloists flew on each side of him in the number 5 and 6 airplanes. Most of the time the tail markings of this aircraft were obscured by exhaust from the leader's plane, a mark of honor.

The end of the A-4's thirteen-year service with the Blue Angels demonstrated how far ahead of his time Ed Heinemann was with his thinking on weight saving in 1951. It was replaced in 1987 by the F/A-18, originally developed by the Northrop Corporation to show how a lightweight fighter using the latest aerodynamics, control systems, and composite materials could perform air-to-air combat and ground-hugging attack missions equally well. As developed into an operational combat aircraft by McDonnell-Douglas, it represents a two- or three-generation leap from the A-4.

The Skyhawk bridged that technological gap, showing how careful attention to detail and single-minded concentration on achieving a specific mission can result in a great, near-timeless airplane.

The A-4C, last of the early-series Skyhawks, carried a gun and two Sidewinder missiles for its own defense, plus up to 18 250lb bombs, single bombs up to 2,000lbs, or any nuclear bombs in the Navy arsenal. *Facing page*: Yankee Station in the Tonkin Gulf, early 1968: Hefting three drop tanks full of fuel, this A-4C is about to be catapulted from the deck of USS Ticonderoga.

This resulted in an increase in gross weight to nearly 15,000lbs. With the new Wright J-65 engine offering 7,700lbs of thrust, a fully loaded Skyhawk would still offer performance better than that of the pure fighters of the time. (Eventually Skyhawks flew at 25,500lbs plus, with engines generating more than 11,000lbs of thrust.)

The Skyhawk's capabilities were such a breakthrough that the El Segundo division of Douglas was awarded a production contract without the usual industrial competition or prototype tests. The Navy's faith was rewarded. The XA4D-1 prototype flew June 22, 1954, from Edwards Air Force Base, in the hands of test pilot Robert Rahn. As part of the trials program, the second preproduction aircraft, piloted by Lt. Gordon Grey, set a new 500-kilometer closed-circuit Class C world's record at an average speed of 695.163 miles per hour on October 15, 1955.

The real value of a breakthrough design in military terms is that it allows plenty of scope for further develop-

MCDONNELL DOUGLAS A-4F SKYHAWK II

Dimensions

Overall wingspan 27ft 6in

Overall length 40ft 1½in

Height 15ft

Engine

One Pratt & Whitney J52-8A turbojet,

9,300lbs static thrust

Weight

Empty 10,465lbs

Loaded (land-based) 27,420lbs

Performance

Maximum speed (clean) 685mph

(4,000lb bombload) 593mph

Range (depending on model

and bombload) 920–2,055mi

Service ceiling (clean) . . . . about 49,000ft

Chance Vought XF8U-1 Crusader

Even among historic prototypes of exotic aircraft, the XF8U-1 Crusader at the Museum of Flight is exceptional. A prototype is a preproduction version of a new type or series of aircraft, built for testing and evaluation. Most prototypes are flown a handful of times—if they don't crash—and are then melted down or relegated to static display.

But the new XF8U-1 Crusader (redesignated F-8 in 1962) was so far ahead of anything else in naval aviation in 1955 that neither the Chance Vought Corporation nor the U.S. Navy's test pilots could stop flying it for more than five years.

"One-X," as this, the first of two Crusader prototypes was referred to at Vought's Dallas plant, flew a total of 507 times, wearing out seventeen Pratt & Whitney J-57 engines, using half a million gallons of fuel, and flying ten times the circumference of the world. Vought's chief test pilot, John Konrad, took it supersonic on its first flight, on March 25, 1955, reaching a speed that has been reported as "about Mach 1.2." For the next five years, the Crusader was airborne an average of once every three days. Fifty pilots flew it. There was no end of new possibilities to be explored.

Facing page: This Crusader shows off the lift-enhancement devices on its multifaceted, many-hinged wing. The entire wing jacks upward at leading edge; inner-wing mounted ailerons act as flaps for takeoff; leading edge slats droop to enable the 1,000mph fighter to generate low-speed lift for takeoff and landing. *This page*: John Konrad folds the landing gear on the first prototype XF8U Crusader, which exceeded the speed of sound on its first flight, March 25, 1955. This early version of one of the outstanding naval fighters of the 1950s and 1960s is on loan to the Museum of Flight from the National Air and Space Museum, Washington, D.C.

It looked so new in 1955 that it still appeared current in 1987, when the last U.S. Navy Crusaders were retired. They continue to fly with the French navy and Philippine air force. A subsonic development of the F-8, the A-7 Corsair II attack plane, is still current with both the Navy and the U.S. Air Force.

The Crusader looked radical from the beginning and still does, mainly because of its wing: it seems to be peeling off the fuselage. As the first supersonic fighter capable of operating from aircraft carriers, the F-8 Crusader was "from the very first a wholly outstanding technical achievement," in the words of English aviation journalist Bill Gunston. Gunston covered the F-8's development firsthand and has written about it many times as an all-too-rare example of a fighter program that succeeded in every respect. In the F-8 chapter of *Early Supersonic Fighters of the West*, published in 1976, Gunston recalls being told by the head of the Navy Bureau of Aeronautics (BuAer), Adm. Jim Russell, that when the bureau had evaluated the eight responses to

its 1952 supersonic fighter competition, the fairly large risk inherent in the Vought entry had not been ignored, "but this design seemed to be the *only* one that would do what everyone in the Navy had been hoping would result from this fighter competition: put the U.S. Navy right in the front rank...."

To say the least. It raised the national air speed record above 1,000 miles per hour for the first time. Comdr. R. W. "Duke" Windsor took it to 1,015.4mph on August 21, 1956, easily surpassing the previous mark of 822mph, set by an Air Force F-100 Super Sabre with a similar engine, and winning the 1956 Thompson Trophy.

On July 16, 1957, Maj. John Glenn, the future astronaut and senator, became the first pilot to fly across the United States faster than the speed of sound, air-refueling his photoreconnaissance Crusader three times en route and taking a continuous strip photograph from Los Angeles to New York.

That December, the Chance Vought Corporation and

Air-to-air photo shows the XF8U's many advanced features, including "the best fighter wing of the 1950s." Set high on the fuselage, it was very strong despite movable surfaces at nearly every edge.

BuAer were awarded the highest aviation honor in America, the Collier Trophy, for their joint success with the Crusader. In March 1958, BuAer in turn presented Vought with the first Navy Certificate of Merit ever awarded an aircraft supplier.

"On top of this," Gunston wrote, the F-8 "was beautiful to fly, was a splendid dogfighter and lacked no armament the pilot wished for. As if all this were not enough, the design, development and clearance for service set a cracking pace"—twenty-one months from detailed design start to first flight—"that no other postwar jet fighter—in the West, at least—has equalled."

The Crusader saved Chance Vought, a company that had specialized in naval aircraft since 1923. In September 1952, when the Navy stated its requirement for a supersonic day fighter, Vought was building the last of 12,000 propeller-driven Corsairs. A design dating from 1938, the Corsair was the first 400mph fighter of World War II. It may also have been the best.

Neither the Navy nor Vought had been able to repeat that success. Vought was a hands-on, engineering-first company whose management and engineering staffs included, by Gunston's count, a higher proportion of ex-fighter pilots than any other large American company: a gung ho outfit game to try almost anything.

Its immediate follow-up to the Corsair was the XF5U, a twin-engine, flying-saucer–shaped prototype with an estimated top speed of 476mph that never flew. Next came Vought's first jet, the underpowered F6U Pirate, but the Corsair was faster. The F7U Cutlass, another radical design with nothing aft of its wings, was slow to develop but did get into production. Future Vought president Paul Thayer qualified for his office in part by twice surviving crashes in F7U prototypes.

The Crusader production program lasted from 1956 to 1965, with 1,259 built. Of those, 446 were stripped and rebuilt to newer standards from 1966 to 1971. Vought built five prototypes of the F8U-3 Super Crusader, which, with a new engine and airframe, was almost twice as fast as the original. The F8U-3s were passed to the National Aeronautics and Space Administration for further testing; a civilian

agency for some years thus operated the only genuine sustainable Mach 2.4 fighters in the West. Next came the A-7 Corsair II. "No other fighter," Vought has claimed, "has ever realized as much growth from its original airframe."

The F-8's most remarkable design feature, its two-way hinged wing, was noteworthy in several respects. To begin with, it was placed at the top of the fuselage, where fighter wings had not appeared in thirty-five years. Since then, high wings have become commonplace. Vought's design team, led by Russ Clark, put the wing there so it could be hinged, and that was done for landing-vision purposes. It could be jacked up twelve degrees at its leading edge so that the airplane could approach a carrier deck with its wing in its highest position and the fuselage nearly level. This enabled the pilot to see the deck.

It was not unusual for the Crusader's wing to be hinged front-to-back, in this case just outboard of its midpoint on each side, so the tips could fold upward to save space on crowded aircraft-carrier decks. But it was highly irregular to fly that way. At least eight times, however, Navy and Marine pilots, sitting far ahead of their wings, inadvertently took off with them folded. The plane would fly almost normally on little more than half its wingspan, aided by the placement of its ailerons inside the hinges.

The wing was as thin as possible without requiring more structural weight to keep it rigid. Still, half the F-8's fuel was carried there, making the wing, aside from its edges and tips, one big fuel tank. The lower fuselage held yet more fuel, a total of 1,400 gallons. The resulting range was impressive for a jet fighter: an F-8 was once flown on internal fuel for three hours and forty minutes. The sealed wing structure was simple but built with extraordinary craftsmanship. The innovative aluminum wing skins had stiffening webs machined into their inside surfaces.

Despite the Crusader's many departures from accepted practice, the project led a charmed life. There were no engine problems. The Pratt & Whitney J-57 powered most of America's early supersonic generation of fighters. Due to the Crusader's aerodynamic refinements, the J-57 made the F-8 faster than its Air Force contemporary, the F-100 Super Sabre. Vought successfully pioneered

Birds of prey: The XF8U prototype's offspring became "The Last Gunfighters" in Vietnam. Bulges below the cockpit are for two of the four cannon.

More than Ten G's

Tactics for photoreconnaissance in Southeast Asia evolved from flying as low as necessary to get the required coverage to remaining above 3,000ft, out of the range of most small arms. However, this altitude placed the photo-plane well within the range of the SA-2 SAM (Surface-to-Air Missile) and deadly AAA (Anti-Aircraft Artillery). Nearly one-quarter of all Crusader losses—twenty RF-8Gs—were photo-birds. One pilot remembers it this way:

Generally, the big threat to the photo pilot was the AAA sector barrage fire over the target. SAMs were rarely fired at us and as far as I know, only one RF-8 was ever attacked by MiGs. The escort shot the MiG and the photo bird returned safely to the ship.

I remember one particular mission where the AAA was really thick over Haiphong. It was a hazy day with a high overcast so the tracers looked like red rain. I got my pictures and decided it was time to turn right. (I always turned right because most guys turned left.)

I was doing about Mach 1.2 as I had come downhill from 35,000ft in [after]burner for the run that was only about two minutes long. I was as scared as I ever have been in my life and really laid in a good turn. Suddenly, I couldn't see very good. My eyes scanned the G meter—

I had tunnel vision really bad—and the needle was sitting on the stop, more than 10 G's. I lost 200 knots in that 100-degree turn while in burner.

With a 6.4-G limit and only 5.1-G rolling, I had really put a hard lick on that bird. Thank goodness Vought built it so tough. I don't know why it didn't come apart and kill me. We found the port outer wing panel was basically destroyed with all the ribs inside broken into little pieces. I still believe that if I hadn't made that turn, I would have been shot down.

… It seemed to me that most of the guys that were shot down were violating some good rule about combat. Never go to the same place twice in the same sorties; never go below 3,500ft; always go as fast as your mission fuel would allow; don't fly through, or near, clouds, and never get caught over an overcast. Also, no matter what you thought about the sortie, "they were always shooting" was a good philosophy; and jink for one gun just as you would for a thousand. Anyone who didn't respect those guys on the ground was stupid and in great peril.

—Capt. Will Gray, VFP-63, Detachment 43, USS
  Coral Sea, 1967, quoted in *Air International.*

the use of titanium for the high-temperature skin areas around the engine by discovering how to spot-weld this brittle but heat-resistant alloy.

The F-8's finest operational hour came not in war but during the uneasy peace of late 1962. High-flying U-2s verified the presence of Soviet missiles in Cuba, but it took RF-8A Crusaders from Navy reconnaissance squadron VFP-62, reinforced by four pilots from Marine squadron VMCJ-2, to provide detailed low-level photographs that told the worldwide public exactly what was going on. They returned from dangerous high-speed night flights over Cuba—an operation code-named "Blue Moon"—with 160,000 negatives. VFP-62 won the first peacetime Presidential Citation, and several pilots were awarded Distinguished Flying Crosses. The last F-8s in U.S. service were photo-birds, retired in March 1987.

The Crusader holds yet another distinction, one that makes it unique in military aviation history. Its basic design has been perpetuated in another aircraft, one similar enough to be its direct offspring but different enough to have a distinct mission.

Son of Crusader is the current Navy–Air Force attack jet, the A-7 Ling-Temco-Vought (LTV) Corsair II, a product of the 1961 merger between Vought and Ling-Temco Electronics, a leading supplier of aircraft navigation, radio, and armament equipment. Naturally, LTV's A-7 had the most advanced radar systems in the world when it was introduced in 1965. The Corsair II is not supersonic, but it does carry bombs weighing one-third more than its equipped empty weight and it delivers them accurately. The A-7 is slower but smarter, and much brawnier, than its dad—evolution at work.

All of its innovations aside, the Crusader's most important stroke of good fortune was its having been designed only months after an aerodynamicist with the National Advisory Committee for Aeronautics, Richard Whitcomb, made an important discovery about supersonic flight. The Air Force's early supersonic fighters were having difficulty breaking through the sound barrier. Whitcomb discovered why. It was known that the shock waves of air created by an object moving at speeds approaching the speed of sound were its main source of drag. But Whitcomb's wind-tunnel research showed that the fuselage and wing of a high-performance aircraft produced the same single shock wave as a fuselage alone.

"In December 1951, while pondering these results," Whitcomb later wrote, "it suddenly occurred to me (much like the proverbial light bulb over a person's head in a comic strip) that the shock wave and the associated drag for the fuselage-wing combination is the same as that for a simple fuselage alone that has the same longitudinal variation of cross-sectional areas as that of the fuselage-wing." In other words, if the design compensated for the bulges created by wings—or cockpit canopies or air intakes—by reducing the circumference of the fuselage at the same points, "substantial reductions of transonic and supersonic drag were achieved." Whitcomb's concept became known as the Area Rule. The Crusader was the first fighter whose fuselage had the Area Rule designed in from the start.

The emphasis on sheer speed at the expense of air combat maneuverability was typical of 1950s fighter designs. It explains why so few of the Crusader's contemporaries lasted very long in first-line service. In response to urgent appeals from U.N. pilots over MiG Alley, North Korea, where the MiG-15 could initiate or break off combat at will, a generation of Western fighters were designed mainly for speed. Some of the same pilots found themselves encountering the MiG-15's successor, the comparatively slow but maneuverable MiG-17, fifteen years later over North Vietnam, in supersonic jets that could not dogfight.

The Crusader was better able to adapt. Most of the other 1950s fighter designs were classic cases of designing for the previous war. An important lesson of Vietnam was the importance of maneuverability in air-to-air combat. Its wing gave the F-8 an edge in that regard. In addition, the F-8 was armed with guns, rather than just air-to-air missiles. By the 1950s, guns were considered obsolete. F-8s, with their ability to fight on after using their missiles, shot down twice as many MiGs in Vietnam as did their successors, the missile-armed F-4C Phantoms, while suffering proportionately lower losses. As Navy and Marine pilots claimed at the time, "When you're out of F-8s, you're out of fighters."

CHANCE VOUGHT F8U-1

Dimensions

Overall wingspan 35ft 8in

Overall length 54ft 3in

Height 15ft 9in

Engine

One Pratt & Whitney J57-P-4

2-shaft turbojet with afterburner, 16,200lbs static thrust

Weight

Empty 15,513lbs

Loaded (max. takeoff, catapult) 27,500lbs

Performance

Maximum speed 1,013mph

Initial climb 21,000ft/min

Service ceiling 42,300ft

Combat radius/mission time 368mi/1.7hr

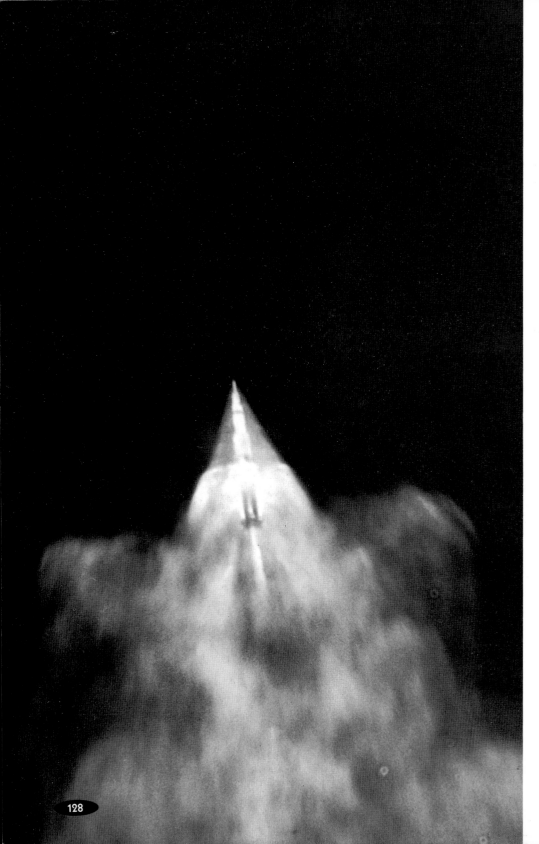

Apollo Command Module

Astronaut Michael Collins was quite happy with his August 1966 assignment to fly the Apollo Lunar Module (LM). The Gemini earth-orbit program was winding down, and assignments for Apollo moon missions were being handed out. Having made two space walks during the Gemini 10 flight only a few weeks before, Collins felt fully qualified to step out of an LM and become one of the first human beings to walk on the moon. After all, he was one of only three Americans with experience of extravehicular (EVA) activity.

Collins threw himself into the unique training program being developed to simulate the delicate process of landing on the lunar surface, in one-sixth of the earth's gravity. But the January 27, 1967, launchpad fire that killed Gus Grissom, Ed White, and Roger Chaffee changed everything. The shock was felt through all levels of the space program. By the end of April, the Apollo Spacecraft Program Office of

Second booster stage fires. The 7.6 million-pound-thrust Saturn V first stage carries the spacecraft to an altitude of 36.3 nautical miles in 2 minutes 40.8 seconds. Less than one second later, this photograph is taken by an EC-135 airplane from 40,000ft. *Facing page*: Apollo 11 liftoff: July 16, 1969, 9:32am EDT. Neil Armstrong, Michael Collins, and Edwin E. "Buzz" Aldrin Jr. go to the moon. Photo shot from the mobile launch tower.

the National Air and Space Administration (NASA) and the contractors for the Apollo Command Module, the Space Division of North American Aviation, had both changed management. Within months North American would become a subsidiary of Rockwell-Standard of Pittsburgh. The Apollo spacecraft would be redesigned for greater safety (a process that, in fact, had begun long before the fire). Meanwhile, all space flights were canceled and the assignments of the thirty astronauts were shuffled.

The third manned Apollo flight, for which Collins had been scheduled as LM pilot in Frank Borman's backup crew, was called off. Collins instead found himself part of the prime crew for a new third mission—as Command Module (CM) pilot. This was a "promotion": chief astronaut Deke Slayton wanted his most experienced hands flying the vehicles that would make critical linkups in space.

In his classic memoir, *Carrying the Fire*, Collins put quotation marks around the word *promotion* because, although he was moving from a backup to a prime crew, and to a more senior position within that, he realized that it would deny him the opportunity to leave his footprints on the moon's Sea of Tranquility. This personnel decision would relegate him to historical-footnote status.

"No LM for me," Collins lamented, "no EVA, no fancy flying, no need to practice in helicopters anymore. Instead I was the navigator, the guidance and control expert, the base-camp operator, the owner of the leaky plumbing—all the things I was least interested in doing."

Leaky plumbing? This referred to problems Collins had spotted on a visit to North American Aviation's plant in Downey, California, where the Apollo CMs were being built. He was not impressed. Faulty plumbing was only one of several potentially hazardous flaws engendered by the CM contractor's "country club" atmosphere, as it was described by a former Convair and General Dynamics manager brought in to shape up North American's operation at the Kennedy Space Center.

Of the five finalist proposals in the grueling competition for the billion-dollar Apollo contract (July 28 to October 9, 1961), the Martin Company's was judged to have the best

THE MUSEUM OF FLIGHT'S SPACECRAFT

The Museum of Flight's Apollo Spacecraft, Command Module 007, was built as a Block 1 Command Module, one of the first batch used for unmanned flights to approximate the dimensions and weight of the real thing, and for manned simulations and testing.

CM 007 was delivered to NASA Houston in March 1966. Its main role was to acquaint the astronauts with the experience of splashdown in the Gulf of Mexico, often bobbing for as long as two hours with three astronauts inside, practicing what were euphemistically referred to as "extended recoveries." So, while this spacecraft never flew, it can be said to have been "flown" as a training vehicle by most of the thirty astronauts active in the space program at the time.

As a vehicle designed previous to NASA's decision to use a "Lunar Orbit Rendezvous" mission mode, it lacked the tip probe for docking with the Lunar Module. It was upgraded to Block 2 status, with the probe, improved hatch, and a more fire-resistant interior, after the 1967 launchpad fire.

This spacecraft, like the ones that went to the moon and back, was capable of withstanding searing temperatures (5,200 degrees F.) on reentry. Its skin consisted of double layers of titanium—a very strong, light metal used for the critical parts in jet engines because of its heat resistance—separated by a corrugated layer for strength and insulation. The blunt base of the spacecraft was covered with ablative tiles, designed to burn away as the spacecraft passed through the earth's atmosphere.

The module did not fare as well on earth, however: after a dozen years of sitting in the open in a public works yard in Fort Worth, CM 007 had water in every hole of its honeycomb structure. Despite the fact that, unlike most aircraft, the Apollo Command Module was not designed to be dismantled, it was fully restored by the Kansas Cosmosphere and Space Center, one of the world's largest space artifact restoration complexes.

The intricacy of the restoration is evident in this view of the gleaming Command Module at the Museum of Flight.

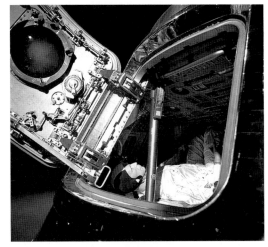

Astronaut dummy shows how limited the space inside was. This was home to three men for most of eight days.

Redesign of the CM hatch was already under way when the January 1967 launchpad fire claimed the lives of Gus Grissom's Apollo 1 crew. The old hatch took 14 minutes to open from outside.

technical approach and the company itself to be the second-best as a business concern. This was no surprise: Martin had devoted 300 people and $3 million to producing a set of recommendations for the moon missions, plans that closely anticipated the form the missions eventually took. The NASA subcommittee evaluating the five companies' administrative capacity ranked North American last.

But North American, builder of the X-15 rocket plane in which Neil Armstrong first encountered the threshold of space in 1962, was a favorite among early proponents of the space program. It was also well thought of by NASA's Space Task Group, which had formulated the general configuration of the Apollo spacecraft, and NASA's senior managers. NASA administrator James Webb followed their advice, overruled the spacecraft Source Evaluation Board's recommendation, and awarded the contract to North American. The night of the contract award, a North American engineer had hats made bearing a NA$A logo.

By the mid-sixties North American was barely able to keep up with the work its reputation attracted. In late 1966, Collins, a recent space traveler overseeing the grooming of his moon ship, found the Downey plant undisciplined and uncraftsmanlike. Assembly workers drank beer during lunch breaks and seemed more interested in their weekend recreational vehicles than in why spacecraft were failing tests.

The investigation board that examined both the burned-out Grissom-White-Chaffee spacecraft and a control specimen concluded that there had been several possible sources of ignition in North American's patched-up wiring; it was not clear which of them had caused the fire. Spacecraft 012, the Grissom crew's CM, had a history of leaky plumbing that had set its preparation back along with that of 014, the Collins vehicle. (Both were Block 1 spacecraft, intended only for earth orbit.) The fire had fed on the 100 percent oxygen atmosphere in the craft, pumped up to 16 pounds per square inch, as specified by NASA. It consumed flammable materials the contractor had been told to minimize. Furthermore, the crew was sealed inside by three separate hatches, the innermost of which opened inward instead of

blowing out. Opening the hatches required outside help and took fourteen minutes. Ironically, the decision to redesign these hatches for the Block 2 spacecraft had already been made.

Most of North American's problems were resolved after a change of management in which William Bergen, a star engineer for thirty-five years at Martin, demoted himself in April 1967 from being head of North American's Space and Propulsion Group to running the Space Division. He appointed Thomas O'Malley, the ten-year Cape Canaveral veteran who had called North American's operation a country club, to professionalize the company's on-site crew. O'Malley in turn restored another Cape veteran to a critical position. This was Guenter Vendt, the tyrannical launchpad overseer of the Mercury and Gemini flights.

Bergen also appointed senior managers to be responsible for each spacecraft in the plant. His old Martin colleague John Healey was to oversee the first Block 2 spacecraft, number 101. "Mr. Spacecraft 101," as Bergen referred to Healey, got NASA to stop demanding continual changes to the vehicles on which North American's reputation now rested.

The effort paid off. The fourteen Apollo spacecraft that followed 101 to the Kennedy Space Center spent, by Collins's calculation, 280 days in space, including the 1975 Apollo-Soyuz rendezvous, without malfunction.

"To me," Collins has written, "the amazing, the incredible, the fantastic (pardon the slip into astronaut parlance) fact is that so few crew mistakes and mishaps have occurred during Gemini and Apollo flights. The opportunities for error are almost limitless, and only superlative design permits virtually error-free operation of a machine as complex as an Apollo Command Module...."

It was in CM 107 that Collins orbited the moon while Armstrong and Aldrin made history on July 20, 1969. The meticulous Guenter Vendt had been mothering 107 for five and a half months before liftoff. CM 107 sat on its own Service Module 107, a 24-foot-7-inch-high cylinder to which the CM was attached until shortly before reentry into earth orbit. The Apollo 11 Service Module weighed 51,243lbs at

launch and contained tanks of helium, fuel, oxygen, and hydrogen, along with the Service Propulsion System (SPS), a 20,500lb-thrust rocket engine. The third-stage Saturn booster engine provided the burn to set sail for the moon, but a three-second blast by the SPS was the ticket for the return trip.

Collins has said that the closest he could come to describing the complexity of the CM's systems was to compare flying it to flying a B-52 bomber. And a B-52, he noted, has a crew of six. Control of the Mercury and Gemini spacecrafts had been somewhat automatic since the focus of the missions was on the physical effects of space flight on the astronauts. But because of its vital rendezvous and docking procedures, the Apollo CM required two-handed flying.

The interior of the CM was battleship gray. It was a densely packed cone, wider, at nearly 13ft, than it was tall, with a total habitable space of 210sq ft. Collins's first impression of it was "those great handfuls of switches. Around four hundred of them, if you include the plungers, the ratchets, the handles, and the knobs." There were 300 of one type of switch alone. Banks of circuit breakers, a cluster of forty-eight warning lights, a pair of artificial horizons, and two computer keyboards all took up space and demanded more-or-less constant attention. Many offered manual control of automatic systems in case something went wrong.

So little space, shared with so much gear, was claustrophobic for three astronauts, dressed much of the time in bulky, stiff spacesuits and cooped up for nearly eight days. A serious, ongoing concern was that, in moving around inside, someone might inadvertently flip a switch, disarming some critical system and creating a time bomb.

Three form-fitting couches were arranged side by side, with the astronauts' backs to the conical spacecraft's base and their knees toward its apex. The couches were suspended independently from the spacecraft shell in case of a hard landing.

Just getting himself situated in his seat before launch was a gymnastic exercise for Collins, who had to grab a bar on the second of the three hatches, swing his legs as far to the right as possible, and shove himself into the seat, pushing his feet into titanium clamps and then resting his head, in its heavy, sealed helmet, on a narrow headrest.

The seats, from left to right, were for the mission commander, Armstrong; the LM pilot, Aldrin; and Collins, the CM pilot. They were set so closely together that elbows rubbed. Underneath was a crawl space where hammocks were rigged for sleeping. Beneath the crew's feet was the equipment bay, with batteries, navigation equipment, an onboard computer not even as powerful as some hand-held calculators of today, and lockers for consumables and rock samples. The intimacy involved in flying for more than a week under these conditions was so intense that by the time earth orbit began, only half an hour into the mission, Collins was already wondering whether Aldrin had gotten up on the wrong side of the bed that morning.

The main instrument panel hung in front of the crew's faces, while smaller ones were set in the bulkheads to Armstrong's left and Collins's right. On previous manned Apollo flights, the CM pilot had occupied the center seat, which allowed easier access to the "astrogation station," where he spent much of his time taking celestial readings. For the first moon-landing mission, however, Collins wanted to operate from both the left- and right-hand seats, the first while flying the CM and the second while monitoring the module's systems. A thin man, Collins figured he could wriggle down to the equipment bay from either side.

To look out the window and fly the Command Module, the pilot had to be in the mission commander's left-hand seat, where the yaw, roll, and pitch controls were. Instead of an airplane's movable flight surfaces, the CM had pairs of small, 100lb-thrust rocket engines called thrusters, most of them distributed around the base of the spacecraft. Pairs on opposite sides of the circumference, for example, set at opposite oblique angles, worked against each other to control roll. By firing in computer-controlled sequences and combinations, most often for split-second bursts, the thrusters enabled the CM pilot to fly the spacecraft with a high degree of accuracy. Collins's final critical task was to hit the ten-mile-wide corridor of the earth's atmosphere at the precise angle that would enable the spacecraft to splash down

Facing page: Apollo 11 crew, in sealed "biological isolation" coveralls to prevent spread of feared moon organisms, in the life raft after splashdown, 11:49am CDT, July 24, 1969, only 12 nautical miles from USS *Hornet*. *This page*: The Apollo 11 Command Module 107 is hoisted aboard the aircraft carrier USS *Hornet*. CM 107 is in the National Air and Space Museum, Washington, D.C.

A Call to Arms

I believe this nation should commit itself to achieving the goal, before this decade is out, of landing a man on the moon and returning him safely to the earth. No single space project in this period will be more impressive to mankind, or more important for the long-range exploration of space; and none will be so difficult or expensive to accomplish.

—President John F. Kennedy, May 25, 1961

within sight of the USS *Hornet*, about eighty miles southwest of the Hawaiian Islands. At that point he would be flying at *36,500 feet per second*. To accomplish this from 230,000 miles out in space required a new order of navigation, computing, and flying precision.

To the left of the mission commander's seat was a throttle in the form of a T-handle that stuck out of the instrument panel. This controlled the direction of movement on any of the three axes. Moving it in or out, up or down, left or right, would move the spacecraft in that direction. (Nearby, at the mission commander's left knee, was the ABORT handle, which could turn the CM into a three-man ejection capsule at any time during the launch.) To the right was the hand controller, more of a double-jointed control stick, which governed the attitude of the spacecraft in relation to any other body.

Collins felt that the CM, shorn of its Service Module just before reentry, flew "like a fighter, reacting vigorously as my right hand keeps it pointed properly." Once back in the atmosphere, where aerodynamics again counted, the CM became a crude form of glider, able to generate lift with its blunt end forward. What had been, eight days before, a 6,000,000lb, 363ft Saturn V rocket stack with enough thrust—7,600,000lbs—to shake the sands four miles from the launchpad was now an 11ft, 11,000lb cone with 1,200lb control thrusters.

Each CM interior was personalized by its crew, mainly with switch labels for hard-to-remember functions, such as S-BAND AUX TO TAPE 90 SEC PRIOR TO DUMP, a reminder to Collins, "to save me some embarrassment in the operation of our tape recorder."

Hundreds of pieces of equipment, from the video camera to exposure meters, were stuck to what small patches of gray wall had been left bare. This haphazard arrangement of miscellaneous items that might be required at any time resulted from the months each crew had spent in simulators, "flying" their missions on the ground. Strips of a relatively new wonder material, Velcro, were used to attach equipment to the spacecraft walls. Dozens of these strips plastered in seemingly random nooks gave the CM a somewhat homey, lived-in look.

To monitor the machine's health, "ask how it's feeling today and take its pulse and temperature and all that stuff," Collins had to be in the right-hand seat. Most of his movements were up and down from there. This was where he sat for liftoff, trading with Armstrong in earth orbit.

Of course, Collins had the CM all to himself while his colleagues made their excursion to the moon's surface. He folded and stored the center couch, glorying in the extra space, and did some thinking. Being there alone made him feel at one point "like the proprietor of a small resort hotel" tidying up for the influx of guests, at another like an anxious mother waiting for her kids to return. Little attention was paid to Collins or his orbiting spacecraft while Neil Armstrong and Buzz Aldrin became immortals below. During the forty-eight minutes of each two-hour moon orbit during which Collins passed over the far side of the moon, he was out of radio contact with anyone, and thus truly alone. He had learned to like it that way: "I enjoyed the fact that I was on one side of this little satellite of our planet and Neil and Buzz were somewhere over on the other side of it, and then there were three billion people a quarter of a million miles away.... I didn't mind being in that corner of the universe alone by myself. I enjoyed that. I wish someone would have communicated with me, but no one did."

Like a Gnat Inside a Blowtorch Flame

William Anders was the Lunar Module pilot on Apollo 8, the first manned flight into lunar orbit, in December 1968. With Frank Borman as mission commander and Jim Lovell as Command/Service Module pilot, Apollo 8 regained the initiative lost after the Apollo 1 fire with an aggressive leap into space, "laying out bread crumbs like Hansel and Gretel for the others to follow," as Anders put it, sending back television pictures of the moon as well as Borman's reading, from seventy miles above the moon, of "In the beginning God created the heaven and the earth...."

There was no way any simulator could duplicate the rattle and roar of a Saturn V rocket at liftoff. The noise was tremendous. Even in our "moon cocoons," closed off from most sounds from the outside, you could hear it and feel it. Despite all the practice, everyone was surprised at what a bone-rattling ride takeoff was. Think of the Saturn V as a car antenna and think of yourself as a bug on top of it and you'll get the picture. A little jiggle on the bottom causes a lot of movement on top. So when those giant rocket engines started adjusting, we started whipping back and forth. At one point it got so bad the thought crossed my mind that the fin of the rocket had caught on to the tower and we were coming down....

The only other hairy moment was reentry because at a speed of thirty-five thousand feet per second, we were moving a helluva lot faster than any previous earth orbit reentry. You could see the flames and the outer skin of the spacecraft glowing; and burning, baseball-size chunks flying off behind us. It was an eerie feeling, like being a gnat inside a blowtorch flame, and I was just hoping those folks down there got all their calculations right.

—William Anders, quoted in "Lunar Reflections," by Jeff Goldberg, *Omni*, July 1989

The Command/Service Module, with Collins waiting inside, is photographed in lunar orbit from the Lunar Module on July 20, 1969, during the moon landing mission. Below is part of the north central Sea of Fertility.

Younger by a Fraction of a Second

Oh, I seem to be spending money a bit more freely now, and I am inclined to put more energy into my family and less into my job, but basically I am the same guy. My wife confirms the fact. I didn't find God on the moon.... But although I may feel I am the same person, I also feel that I am different from other people. I have been places and done things you simply would not believe, I feel like saying: I have dangled from a cord a hundred miles up; I have seen the earth eclipsed by the moon, and enjoyed it. I have seen the sun's true light, unfiltered by any planet's atmosphere. I have seen the ultimate black of infinity in a stillness undisturbed by any living thing. I have been pierced by cosmic rays on their endless journey from God's place to the limits of the universe, perhaps there to circle back on themselves and on my descendants. If Einstein's special theory is true, my travels have made me younger by a fraction of a second than if I had always stayed on the earth's surface.... It is perhaps a pity that my eyes have seen more than my brain has been able to assimilate or evaluate, but like the Druids at Stonehenge, I have attempted to bring order out of what I have observed, even if I have not understood it fully.

—Michael Collins, *Carrying the Fire*

APOLLO COMMAND MODULE

Height 10ft 7in

Diameter 12ft 10in

Weight (including crew) 13,000lbs

Weight (splashdown) 11,700lbs

Weight (combined Command/Service

Modules) 65,000lbs

Weight of Lunar Module at linkup 33,000lbs

Boeing 747

By the time its chief engineer, Joseph Sutter, realized the 747 was going to be overweight, the most expensive gamble in the Boeing Company's history was teetering on the brink of disaster. Sutter, who had been heavily involved with every Boeing jetliner, had never found himself in a jam like this.

It was the spring of 1967. The project had defied the odds since its beginning in late 1965. It had evolved out of a seemingly impossible U.S. Air Force requirement for the biggest transport plane yet conceived in the West, the CX-HLS (later to become the C-5A). Boeing had lost the contest to Lockheed, but to capitalize on its investment in the CX-HLS, the company decided to put a commercial transport of almost the same size in the air in thirty-two months.

A little more than halfway along, this schedule was looking overly ambitious. Many airlines believed the 747 was going to be too big for them to operate profitably anyway. Its engines were not ready. Maybe Boeing had finally bitten off more than it could chew.

Not only did Boeing have to build the world's biggest airliner, it had to build a place to build it. A separate division, the 747 Division, was created solely for the jumbo jet and its factory. The 747 plant, set on 783 acres north of Seattle at Everett, Washington, became the world's largest enclosed space, with its own rail spur and custom-built railway cars.

Just thinking about the early days of the 747 program "brings sweat to the palms of my hands," Boeing's then-president, William Allen, said years later.

The company's net worth in 1967 was about $750 million. Getting the plane Boeing was calling the Superjet into production was going to cost at least that much—in effect, Boeing was betting the company on the 747. Sixteen major subcontractors, spread from California to Northern Ireland, were sharing the risk, which totaled close to a billion dollars.

The 747 prototype has enjoyed a long and useful flight-test career. This 1973 takeoff was accomplished with 143,000lbs of thrust.

OTHER AERIAL GIANTS

The 747 is not the largest aircraft in civil aviation history. It is only the first of its size to succeed. Earlier attempts to build giant aircraft were all frustrated by the state of engine technology.

Germany's 55-ton Dornier Do X flying boat of 1929, with its 157ft 5in wingspan, needed twelve engines to take off from even the longest stretches of water. They were set back-to-back in six nacelles mounted on struts above its wing, six to pull and six to push. These engines were constantly changed, from air-cooled radials to water-cooled V-12s, in the search for reliability. A total of three were built.

The Russian Tupolev ANT-20 *Maxim Gorki*, which first flew in 1934, had six engines on the leading edges of the 206ft 11in wing, and then, as if those weren't quite enough, another two were mounted back-to-back on struts above the fuselage, with spaces in the wings and between the overhead engines for mechanics to do in-flight maintenance.

Aero-engines had come a long way by 1944, but the wartime Hughes *Spruce Goose* flying boat needed eight of the largest radial engines ever built—3,000-horsepower, twenty-eight-cylinder Pratt & Whitney Wasp Majors, the most powerful piston engines in the world—to rise even as briefly as it did from Long Beach Harbor in 1947. At 320ft it had the longest wingspan of any aircraft ever built. The single example built flew that one time, just so Howard Hughes could prove it would.

Above left: A 1929 photo of the German Do X, fresh from a 160-passenger flight. *Left*: The Do X: twelve engines, 48.5 tons. *Facing page*: Angered by congressional questions about his World War II defense contracts, Howard Hughes took what was unofficially named the Hughes Hercules, but popularly (and inaccurately) called the *Spruce Goose,* to Long Beach, assembled it, invited reporters aboard for a taxi trial, and took off—by accident, he claimed.

The day after the outcome of the C-5A competition was announced, Boeing formed its 747 team, headed by Maynard Pennell and Sutter. Pennell had been responsible for the Boeing 707 and was by then director of engineering for the Boeing Commercial Airplane Company. Sutter's previous design credit (along with Jack Steiner) was the shapely 737.

That same day, October 1, 1965, Pan American World Airways, the launch customer, began discussing its requirement for a new-generation long-range airliner with Boeing. Pan Am had a long history of commissioning daring new airliner designs from Boeing, from the 314 Clipper flying boat to the pressurized Stratocruiser, the P-307 Stratoliner, and the first American jet-powered transport, the 707. Now it wanted a big airplane that would save the airline thirty to thirty-five percent on its costs per seat-mile—a quantum leap in jet transport efficiency—on Pan Am's transoceanic routes.

One of the first calculations of Sutter's C-5A-747 team was that using the C-5A-type engines would enable them to design an airliner that would use twenty-five percent less fuel. That and the additional size of a wide-body would meet Pan Am's difficult target. By the end of October, the focus of discussions between Pan Am and Boeing had moved to a two-deck airplane, similar to the old Model 377 Stratocruiser, that could carry 350 passengers at 600 miles per hour. By then Boeing had produced 200 variations of the 747 fuselage on paper.

This second option was a double-bubble fuselage cross section, like the Stratocruiser's, tucked in a little more than halfway up the fuselage, with wings set high on the lower bubble. The wing carry-through structure would separate the lower deck into two compartments.

Both Boeing and Pan Am liked this arrangement. But some airlines were skeptical about the safety of the top-deck passengers in an emergency (and the bottom-deck passengers in a watery ditching). Edward Wells, Boeing's senior executive in charge of design, vetoed the double-decker on those grounds.

Like most great designs, the final one was simplicity itself. Boeing believed the 747 would soon be boxed in by the cheaper stretched Douglas DC-8, and the supersonic transport, or SST, that Boeing was then competing to produce. (Boeing won, but the government-funded project was canceled in 1971.) Both customer and supplier thought the 747 should be easily convertible to a cargo plane (two of Pan Am's originally ordered 747s were cargo versions). It helped that the width of fuselage needed to accommodate two aisles and nine seats (with an option for ten) that Pan Am wanted was the same size as a circle drawn around two standard 8-by-8-by-20-foot cargo containers placed side by side.

As designed so far, the 747 was typically Boeing: very big, strong, and fast. Its basic structural integrity came from the rigid wing box, a panel running almost the length of its wingspan. The fore and aft vertical walls of this box were the main wing spars. The box was sealed to form the four main fuel tanks. It was attached to the center fuselage section by the front four of five forged and machined circular fuselage formers; the fifth carried the loads from a keel beam supporting the rearmost pair of the unique four-leg landing gear system. The engine pylons were attached to the front and back spars by bolts designed to break away under impact, allowing the engine and its carriers to break away cleanly without damaging the fuel tanks or severing control or hydraulic lines (as has happened with other airliners).

Much of the Boeing 727 wing, a masterpiece of its kind, was incorporated into the 747, including its triple-slotted flaps. Five times the wind-tunnel testing as had ever been done on a Boeing design was performed. Two 9ft scale models, each of which cost as much as a DC-6 airliner, were used.

Paring weight from these critical frame elements would be a delicate process: ounce by ounce, millimeter by millimeter. If the 747 could not retain its structural integrity while meeting its performance guarantees, the entire billion-dollar program would be in jeopardy. During 1967 the first metal for the prototype was being cut, and parts were being shipped to the new plant in Everett. The first production activity began in January, and the mammoth assembly hall was due to be activated in May.

At this critical moment the weight crisis took hold. The airframe was 16,000 pounds over estimates, and the interior furnishings nearly 31,000lbs over. Those amounts may not appear to be much on a leviathan designed to gross 680,000lbs. But each of those extra pounds, if not removed, would have to be subtracted from the airplane's projected 192,000lb payload—the maximum revenue-earning weight that the 747 would carry.

The Sutter team tried both to cut weight *and* compensate for whatever weight might remain. Under a "Lift and Thrift" program, everyone associated with the 747 was encouraged, and often paid bonuses, for weight-saving suggestions. Some structural strengthening was done to allow the takeoff weight to increase to 710,000lbs without compromising payload.

That would require increased power. Pratt & Whitney was asked to accelerate development of its JT9D turbofan—then producing about 41,000lbs thrust—to provide 43,500lbs, with an option for a 45,000lb version.

Finally, Boeing tried a tactic it had resorted to previously when it had found itself at an engineering dead end:

Facing page top: Hand-building the 747 upper-fuselage mockup, January 10, 1968; *bottom*: Burp! The 747 nose mockup swallows a cargo container. The plane's characteristic upper-deck bubble put the pilots entirely above the cargo area. *Above*: An early 747 cockpit: It looks modern enough, but later 747-400 models had digital readouts with functions grouped on screens, lessening the workload and reducing the cockpit crew by one—the flight engineer.

747-200B MAKE OR BUY

AERONCA
AUBURN
BOEING, CANADA/WINNIPEG*
BOEING, PORTLAND
CLEVELAND PNEUMATIC
EVERETT
FUJI, JAPAN**
HAWKER de HAVILLAND, AUSTRALIA**
HEATH TECHNA
KAWASAKI, JAPAN**
MITSUBISHI, JAPAN**
NORTHROP
PRATT & WHITNEY
GENERAL ELECTRIC
ROLLS ROYCE
ROCKWELL INTERNATIONAL
ROHR INDUSTRIES
WICHITA
BRITISH AEROSPACE/EVERETT
SHORT BROS & HARLAND
SIERRACIN
PPG INDUSTRIES
TRIPLEX (PRIME)
VERTOL
VOUGHT SYSTEMS
WICHITA

*WING/BODY FAIRING AT NORTHROP PRIOR
TO C/L 702
**WING FLIGHT CONTROLS AT FAIRCHILD
PRIOR TO C/L 702

June, 1986

The 747 started out as a 16-company joint venture. In 1986, this was the breakdown of parts and sections from Boeing divisions and subcontractors.

the company decided to compete with itself. Management set up a 100-worker unit under Pennell, Sutter's boss, to work independently of the regular 747 team and second-guess its strategic decisions.

"The 747, at this stage, became a kind of competition between the two groups," Sutter later explained.

"The top-side thinking was that, maybe, we guys who had been working so close to the project were running a little scared. Maybe we were doing something all wrong, tightening up, paying too much attention to the urgency of the scheduling program, any number of things. Maybe what was needed was a fresh start with guys who could hit the thing with less inhibitions."

Two of the solutions involved more pioneering materials technology. The landing gear beams (which carry the landing loads) were fabricated from solid titanium—the largest items ever made from that light but expensive metal. The big fairing that smooths airflow over the wing-fuselage junction is made of Nomex-impregnated paper, a material developed for its flameproof qualities for internal applications but used on non-load-bearing outer surfaces.

The strain on the 747's engine program began to show once the prototype got into the air. It took time to spot the

problem. Although the prototype flew February 9, 1969, and had its first flight cut short by a minor forward-flap glitch, the second flight six days later went well. Handling and systems checks indicated that Sutter and his staff had created, as chief project pilot Jack Waddell put it, "a pilot's dream." Turbulence had been reported in the Puget Sound area, but none of the three on board—Waddell, copilot Brien Wygle, or Jess Wallick, the flight engineer—noticed it. Drag was lower than anticipated. Cruise performance and fuel consumption were much better.

The 747 had been made possible by the development of the most powerful aircraft engines yet devised, engines that offered unprecedented increases in power, fuel economy, and quietness. They did this by taking in two to three times the volume of air of previous turbojet engines—enough to fill a cathedral every two seconds—by means of a fan mounted just inside the engine intake and driven by the jet. This fan amounts to a huge forty-six-blade propeller. Its durability at very high temperatures was one result of the huge advance in materials technology underwritten in part by the Air Force's C-5A project.

Since most of the air taken in passes unburned around the compression-combustion apparatus, these powerplants are called "high bypass" turbofans. The 747's Pratt & Whitney JT9Ds have 8ft-diameter inlets, twice the size of those on similar-type engines on later 707s. In 1969, when the 747 first flew, the fastest fighter planes in the world were powered by one or two engines with static thrust power ratings approaching 20,000lbs each. The 747's four turbofans each develop more than twice that.

P&W had guaranteed the performance of its engines before they had been thoroughly proven, something the company had never done before. It had done so to get the 747 work in place of General Electric, winner of the C-5A engine contract. GE, the leader in turbofan technology, believed Boeing's tight schedule left insufficient time for development of the revolutionary engines, which would have stricter durability, pollution, and quietness requirements than the military versions for the C-5A. So it should have come as no surprise that the JT-9Ds were not quite ready when the 747 was rolled out.

The problem was low power in the takeoff and climb modes, and resulting high fuel consumption. These shortcomings became apparent during the most intensive flight test program ever, in which the prototype and four early-production airplanes flew 1,500 hours of precertification testing in 1969. Both were serious enough to threaten Boeing's overall performance guarantees.

The two companies shared the blame. Originally, Boeing had hung the engines from their pylons by two attachments. This was a significant and costly mistake. The phenomenal increase in power over anything seen before distorted the engine casings when throttle was applied, causing a general distortion of tolerances within the engine and a loss of thrust when it was needed most.

By the time a new engine frame and internal changes solved the problem of power loss on takeoff, twenty-two 747s had come off the line without engines and were jokingly referred to as "the world's biggest gliders." The program was weeks behind schedule, and interest charges and modification costs were adding up to $2.5 million a week. There was no cash flow from the airplanes awaiting engines.

All of which pales to insignificance in the light of two decades of steady sales, now at 950, of nine distinct 747 models, including 747-400s capable of flying 8,000 miles nonstop. How much of an advantage Boeing gained by being first with a wide-body jumbo jet is difficult to determine because not only was Boeing first, it was also in a class by itself for maximum payload and range.

The McDonnell Douglas DC-10 did not fly until the end of August 1970, while Lockheed's L-1011 TriStar flew that November. Neither is in production today.

The 747 prototype, based at Boeing's Flight Test Center, Boeing Field, has been active as a test aircraft for nearly twenty years. It has flown with several engine and interior configurations and numberless avionics setups, including the sophisticated Full-Flight-Regime-Autothrottle and National Command Center electronics suites. It will likely be retired to the Museum of Flight when—and if—its usefulness to ongoing test programs declines. For a design thought to be a lame duck awaiting the SST, an airplane likely to be produced into the twenty-first century is more than a milestone design. It is a monument.

First shock of landing is absorbed by angled landing-gear wheel bogies.

ORIGINS OF THE 747:
THE C-5A CONTEST

During the early 1960s, the U.S. Air Force demonstrated to NATO its ability to move a division of troops to Europe in just under three days. In so doing, the Air Force proved to itself that its transport planes were almost wholly inadequate for the task. To begin with, the mechanized division taken from Texas to West Germany arrived without its heavy equipment.

No aircraft in the inventory of the Military Air Transport Service (MATS) could carry tanks. Older transports could not fly the Atlantic nonstop. Newer ones could, but only by carrying less. The only fast, long-range transports available were C-135s, cargo versions of the civil Boeing 707. The handful available in 1963 carried twenty percent of the total tonnage, but they could not load bulky items. MATS's newest transport, the Lockheed C-141A Starlifter, was fast but had less internal cargo space than some of the planes it was to replace.

The Air Force spent most of 1962 studying both its projected transport role and its needs from 1970 onwards. After a further year of definition, a requirement emerged for a transport that could carry 180,000lbs of cargo over a 5,000-mile radius, or a smaller load for the unheard-of dis-tance of 12,000 miles, unrefueled. It would require turbofan engines that existed only on paper at the time, and very advanced wings that would use air bled from the engines to control the airflow over them.

The manufacturers — and some Air Force officials — felt this to be unrealistic. So MATS left it to the manufacturers to decide how to meet the specs for the CX-HLS, for Cargo Experimental–Heavy Logistics System. Detailed studies by Boeing, Lockheed, and Douglas, and two engine suppliers, Pratt & Whitney and General Electric, were funded, and money set aside to buy fifty-eight of what the Air Force was now calling the C-5A.

By then the required payload was up to a quarter-million pounds, and a number of other difficult conditions had been set, such as the ability to land and take off from unprepared fields without breaking up the surface. This last was a formidable requirement: The C-5A was twice the size of any airplane then in existence. Boeing called its effort "the big-plane exercise."

The company's research into meeting the soft-field demand involved re-engineering the 707 prototype with eight-wheel, wide-track main landing gear legs to spread the load. One result of this research is the 747's distinctive cranked four-wheel bogies, or pairs of wheels, which hang down at a fifty-three-degree angle to allow some tires to absorb initial landing impact before others touch down.

A Boeing publicity photo from the mid-sixties shows four employees with more than 150 cardboard boxes containing the company's top-secret submission to the C-5A evaluators. The pared-down engineering summary was thicker than the New York City phone book.

The outcome was one more example in Boeing's history of short-term pain leading to long-term gain. Boeing's design was judged the best, but it came with the highest price tag and lost the competition. Judging by the overruns that plagued the winning Lockheed C-5A program, Boeing may have had a clearer idea than anyone else of how much building such an airplane would cost.

THE 747'S IMPACT

Fourteen stewardesses! Upper-deck lounge and bar! Spiral staircase! Vertical tail six stories high! Two-inch-wider economy seats! Twelve restrooms and six movie screens! Six hundred miles per hour: London thirty minutes closer than ever before!

We forget how primitive life in the air was before the 747 appeared in 1969. We forget how astounding those features seemed at the time, how the idea of carrying nearly five hundred passengers 4,000 miles on a single nonstop flight has become routine. The latest 747-400 model flies almost double that nonstop, 7,300 nautical miles — Chicago to Seoul, London to Tokyo.

Everyone involved with the 747 project became infected with the idea of sheer bigness. The new Boeing would be one-third again as large as the biggest jet then flying, the eight-engine B-52 bomber. It would be two and a half times the size of Boeing's biggest commercial jet, the intercontinental 707.

Pan American World Airways, the launch customer with an initial order for twenty-five 747s at $525 million — then the largest order for a single type in commercial aviation history — claimed it was "pioneering a whole new era in air transportation, introducing the *spacious* age!"

The 747 changed everything it touched. John F. Kennedy International Airport in New York City jury-rigged two temporary gates for Pan Am's 747s in 1970 while a new $70 million terminal was under construction. Washington's Dulles International Airport, widely referred to before as a white elephant, was suddenly too small. The catch-up capital requirement to accommodate the 747 at U.S. airports alone was estimated at $8.7 billion by 1975, and eighty percent of that was for huge hub terminal areas.

"The old techniques for handling baggage, serving meals and even cleaning out the ashtrays have proved obsolete for the 747," *The Wall Street Journal* warned prospective passengers in 1969. Nevertheless, when Pan Am ran an ad inviting passenger reservations for the first airline flight of the 747, more than 2,500 persons responded.

"The development of this airplane," Boeing president T. A. Wilson said on the occasion of its first flight, "is one of the most gigantic non-governmental undertakings in American history."

The 747 did more than rebuild airports and revolutionize air travel; it reorganized the aircraft industry worldwide. Boeing had already seized the lead in airliner sales from Douglas Aircraft at the dawn of the jet airliner age with the 707. The company consolidated its hold on the global airliner market during the next ten years with the medium-range tri-jet 727 (which flew February 9, 1963) and the short-haul 737 twin (April 9, 1967).

This family approach encouraged airlines to buy Boeing jumbo jets instead of those from Douglas and Lockheed. The net effect was to drive Lockheed out of the wide-body transport market, while McDonnell Douglas attempted to rebound from its luckless DC-10 experience with its MD-11. This shakeout left the remaining commuter wide-body segment to Europe's Airbus Industries and its A-300 series.

Arrival of the Spacious Age: 747 rollout at Everett, September 30, 1968.

Spreading the load: Four four-wheel main landing-gear bogies carry most of the 747's 435-ton maximum takeoff weight.

BOEING 747

Dimensions

Overall wingspan 195ft 8in

Overall length 231ft 4in

Height 63ft 5in

Engines

For first flight tests: four Pratt & Whitney JT9D-1 high-bypass turbofans rated at 41,000lbs. First Pan Am examples used JT9D-3As, 43,500lbs. Latest 747-400 can take P&W 4000, General Electric CF6-80, or Rolls-Royce RB-211 engines: 56,000–58,000lbs thrust at sea level.

Weight

Basic operating 367,900lbs

Maximum payload 158,600lbs

Maximum takeoff 710,000lbs

Maximum takeoff (747-400) 870,000lbs

Performance

Maximum speed (at 30,000ft) . . . . . . Mach .9, or 608mph

Best economy cruise 580mph

Cruise ceiling 45,000ft

Range 4,985mi

Range (747-400) 7,300mi

Rutan VariViggen

The VariViggen homebuilt sport plane was Burt Rutan's first step as an airplane designer toward conceiving the *Voyager*, in which his elder brother, Richard, and Jeana Yeager flew around the world nonstop in 1986—"on a single tank of gas," as the Rutans like to put it. The Rutan trademark is aircraft design for very specific purposes, and there has never been a more singular goal than the one for which *Voyager* was built.

So it was with the VariViggen. "I wanted an aircraft for myself as close to a modern fighter as possible—something like the F-104 or F-4. I wanted a big stick, an array of buttons, high rate of roll—a real 'macho machine' where I'd really feel like I was flying a Century Series fighter," Burt Rutan told Don and Julia Downie, authors of *A Complete Guide to Rutan Aircraft*.

It comes as a surprise that an individual can envision something like that these days. *And* build it. Aircraft design has become more and more a task for the engineering staffs of corporate giants.

But the industrialization of aviation opened up fertile territory for imaginative, low-volume builders like the Rutan Aircraft Factory, or "RAF," in Rutan family terminology. The Rutans are the most successful of these cottage industries operating out of hangars. They are idea generators, inventors who will try to make almost anything fly. The aviation pioneers of today.

Burt Rutan founded Scaled Composites Inc. in the early 1980s to build and flight-test preprototype large-scale flying models of new designs for other companies. (This method is much cheaper than flight-testing full-sized prototypes.) Scaled Composites became a subsidiary of Beech Aircraft Corporation after Rutan conceived the new Beech Starship executive transport, designed it with Beech engineers, and flight-tested an 85 percent-scale proof-of-concept model built by Scaled on August 29, 1983.

Rutan learned the technique of model flight-testing with his one-fifth-scale model of the VariViggen during the late 1960s. He did his own wind-tunnel tests on the plane by clamping an instrumented model to the car-top luggage carrier of his 1966 Dodge Dart and driving at 80 miles per hour through the night. He was never arrested for speeding.

The VariViggen was more than the younger Rutan brother's stepping-stone into aviation history. It is an aircraft that has brought personal flying within the reach of many thousands of ordinary people. *The Encyclopedia of Home-built Aircraft* calls the VariViggen's construction methods "conventional to most of today's amateur-built aircraft" and estimates building time at 1,700 work-hours. To the home-builders of the Experimental Aircraft Association (EAA), Burt Rutan was a hero long before he sketched out *Voyager* on a table napkin at the Mojave Inn.

"We could see he was serious," Dick Rutan wrote in *Voyager*, his account, written with copilot Jeana Yeager, of their 1986 nonstop, around-the-world flight. At first Dick thought the idea "belonged to the same category of things as flying to Mars—some wacko engineering notion."

"Burt has a freedom of thought that makes him successful," Dick writes. "That is part of his genius. He doesn't constrain his thought processes with old ideas, but takes a fresh look at every problem, and it is amazing to see him work."

Burt Rutan has a lot in common with a number of other American aviation originals. Like Orville Wright, he has a brother on hand as constant critic, competitor, and, finally, in his role as *Voyager* pilot, colleague. Dick, five years his brother's senior, finished first in his class at Air Force flight school and was a three-tour fighter pilot in Vietnam. He ended up doing dangerous solo spotter flights over North Vietnam in F-100s, finding targets for air strikes.

Dick joined RAF in 1978, after being passed over for a squadron command. He hated working for his younger brother. Burt, in turn, was concerned about the threat posed by Dick's aerobatics at fly-ins, and the record attempts in Rutan designs that Burt felt jeopardized RAF's reputation for safety. The *Voyager* project presented them with a mutual goal that kept them together through the 1980s.

Like Jean Roché and his Aeronca C-2, Burt Rutan designed the VariViggen in his spare time while working at

Facing page: Three of Burt Rutan's designs. From the top: VariEze is built from glass/foam/glass composite materials and can do 200mph with only 100hp; VariViggen, Rutan's original design for a two-seat touring/sport plane built of plywood; and, foreground, the Long EZ, which set speed and distance records of up to 2,000km at more than 200mph in the hands of Dick Rutan and Jeana Yeager in 1982. *This page*: Mike Melvill, builder and pilot of the Museum of Flight's Vari-Viggen. Note the twin fins, fighter-type blown canopy, and canard foreplanes, a Wright brothers feature repopularized by the Rutan Aircraft Factory.

the Air Force's test center, in this case Edwards Air Force Base. While there he was credited with being "the man who saved the F-4 Phantom program" by writing a manual on how to recover the big fighter-bomber from a spin. The research involved ejecting from a doomed, spinning F-4.

Like many visionaries, Rutan is far more interested in solving engineering problems than in manufacturing. He doesn't mass-produce airplanes; he publishes plans for homebuilders to construct tested, proven designs. Long before he finishes the current project, his mind is occupied with the next one. As Burt and his wife, Carolyn, labored over drawings for the sixty-three-page book of VariViggen plans (price: $51) that would be the main salable product of his labors on the design since 1969, he wrote home, "Well, I guess I'm itching to get started on another airplane of my own...."

The VariViggen prototype, now in the EAA museum in Oshkosh, Wisconsin, was painted in the colors of the Thunderbirds, the U.S. Air Force's aerobatic display team. It soon became known as "Thunder Chicken." It won the coveted EAA award for Outstanding New Design at the EAA Fly-in at Oshkosh in 1974.

With its twin rudders and broad, short wing, the VariViggen reminds people of the newest generation of fighters. Rutan was wise to choose for his general configuration model the Swedish Saab JA-37 Viggen ("thunderbolt"). The Viggen, like all Saab jet fighters since 1955, has a triangular, or delta, wing.

Many early supersonic types, including the Century Series Convair F-102 and F-106, used delta wings because their broad expanse generates high lift and they can be built super-thin for low drag and high speed. Because delta wings usually have their trailing edges well back along an aircraft's axis, their flaps and ailerons can substitute for elevators, saving the weight and drag of a horizontal tail.

In fighters, these advantages are obtained at the cost of long takeoff runs, less agility, and reduced spin recovery. The drawbacks can be mitigated with canards: smaller horizontal flight surfaces ahead of the wings to control the aircraft's pitch.

The Saab Viggen, which first flew in 1967, has both delta wings and delta-shaped canards. The canards enable the Viggen to take off and land in a little more than 1,500 feet, making it one of the few Short Take-Off and Landing (STOL) fighters in the world. In wartime, that capability would enable the Viggen to operate from highways after major airfields had been bombed. The VariViggen applies the same concepts to a pure sports plane.

The VariViggen is a homebuilt that resembles a jet. The owner's manual points out that "the entire cockpit layout and canopy are closer to a modern fighter than any light aircraft." Unlike fighters, however, it is inherently stable and spinproof. It can easily be flown nose-high, as Burt Rutan discovered during the initial flight tests in early April 1972, and is therefore very safe in the takeoff and landing cycles.

The VariViggen's aerodynamics were revolutionary then and remain exceptional now: all the flight control surfaces work in an unusual degree of harmony, with two or more handling the same airflow to achieve phenomenal agility. It can turn at practically any angle of attack with only its rudders or ailerons. Crashing a VariViggen would require a deliberate act of suicide.

By the standards of his more recent designs, Burt Rutan feels that the VariViggen is crude in both its materials and its proliferation of flight surfaces. The subsequent Vari-Eze and Long EZ tailless models and the twin-engine push-

Facing page: Mike Melvill flies a VariViggen in loose formation with the VariEze. *Above:* "I wanted an aircraft for myself as close to a modern fighter as possible." The Saab JA-37 Viggen was Burt Rutan's general configuration model for the VariViggen.

Landed Just at Sunset

Very seldom does the chief engineer of a new airplane do his own flight tests these days. Burt Rutan has flown flight tests at Edwards AFB in F-4 Phantoms, but he was putting as much of himself on the line as any military test pilot when he took off in the VariViggen prototype. More, in fact. If the VariViggen didn't fly, it was not only Rutan's hide but his pride. His wallet was also at stake: he had quit the Air Force and joined Bede Aircraft of Newton, Kansas, where he did the VariViggen flight testing.

It is revealing that, as its designer, he remembers when it was rolled out, February 27, 1972, better than when it first took flight, "about the first of April, '72."

… I found the airplane to be very maneuverable on the ground. Its geometry is such that it can be nosed up to within three feet of a hangar, turned, and taxied away without ground assist. I can easily see the wingtips and rudders from the cockpit and due to its short and low wings, it can be taxied between and around other airplanes much easier than conventional aircraft.…

Another initial problem involved the engine. I had smooth operation up through about half throttle, then the engine would quit if the throttle were advanced further. I found I could get ⅔ throttle if I leaned the mixture, but that was all.…

After more tries to get the engine to run properly, I convinced myself that it would run reliably up to ⅔ throttle and that's enough to fly. I set up a movie camera, run by Les Berven, our BD-5 Test Pilot, got the wife and kids out to the airport and started my first high speed taxi tests. I started at 35 knots and made successively faster taxi·runs in five-knot increments, checking controllability.

The nose gear left the ground on the 45 knot run and I found it very easy to hold the nose off in any attitude I wanted.… On the next run at 50 knots, I exercised the ailerons to see if it would rock while light on the main gear with the nose up. To my surprise, I found myself slightly off the ground rocking the tires on the runway! I decided the next run would be a brief flight down the runway at about 3 feet altitude…. The feel of all three axes was solid and smooth—and I was one happy guy! The landing was a grease job but in my relief I let the nose down hard in one of the ruts in the runway and the nose gear collapsed.… Faced with 90 minutes of daylight remaining and very still, no-wind conditions, I decided to make a quick repair and fly. Within a half hour I was on the end of the runway and setting my ⅔ throttle and lean mixture for takeoff.

… Takeoff and climb were normal and a very strange feeling came over me as I cleared the end of the runway. The air was absolutely still and there I was climbing straight ahead. I had waited a long time for this moment, but somehow it felt like I was on my first solo.

I leveled off at 1,500ft AGL and performed some stability checks—static and dynamic—and pleased with the results, I proceeded to do sideslips and maneuvering turns. I set the reflex at several positions and slowed up to full aft stick to check low speed handling. Again the aircraft felt solid, while still responsive—particularly in roll. So much for the work. I moved in to the Cessna [chase plane] for some pictures, then made a low pass down the runway and landed just at sunset after 50 minutes of enjoyable flying.

—Burt Rutan, quoted in *Sport Aviation*, August 1973

pull Defiant offer much-improved efficiency. The VariEze is available in kit form. The *Voyager*, of course, epitomizes fuel efficiency in the cruise mode but is virtually useless for anything but round-the-world flights.

During the nearly twenty years since Burt Rutan first flew the VariViggen, he has stepped into a vacuum left by the stagnation of private aviation since the 1950s. Very little has appeared in the way of exciting and affordable private aircraft since the Beech Bonanza of 1946. Sales of private aircraft actually declined during the 1980s because of the cost to manufacturers of liability insurance. The net result for the weekend flyer is a limited range of mediocre-performing aircraft carrying price tags that have tripled in ten years to $30,000 or more.

For half that amount—and perhaps as much as six years of spare time spent in the garage—the private flyer can build any one of four Rutan designs and have an efficient, roomy, record-breaking, fun-to-fly two-seater airplane designed by a state-of-the-art aero-engineer.

Burt Rutan has begun to have a much wider influence on general aviation with the introduction of canard flight surfaces on large civil aircraft. Canards originated with the Wright brothers' 1903 Flyer, but were banished to the back when tractor engines, located at the front of an aircraft, began to replace pushers after 1910. On prop-driven aircraft, though, tail-mounted elevators must cope with vortexes from the wings and propwash, while canards can bite into clean air.

Rutan originated the design of Beech Aircraft's revolutionary Model 2000 Starship I, which is now in production and features vertical "tipsails" at the wingtips for directional stability and canards for pitch control. Built from epoxy-graphite composites similar to those from which the *Voyager* was fabricated, the Starship is powered by twin turboshafts mounted on the wings as pushers.

Combining a pitch-control device from the first powered and manned aircraft and built from the latest materials, the Starship represents Beech's commitment to the next fifty years of flight. And one more innovation from Burt Rutan.

RUTAN VARIVIGGEN

Dimensions

Overall wingspan	19ft
Overall length	20ft
Height	5ft 6in

Engine

One Lycoming 150hp, aft-mounted in pusher configuration

Weight

Empty	1,020lbs
Loaded	1,700lbs

Performance

Maximum speed	165mph
Cruise	150mph
Ceiling	14,900ft
Range	300mi

Lear Fan Model 2100

William Powell Lear Sr. started working on his most ambitious aircraft project when he was seventy-five—late, even in the life of a genius. He used up the last of his millions and the last of his life on the Lear Fan, his most beautiful and costly creation.

From its needle-nosed flight-test instrument probe to its unique Y-tail and its pusher prop powered by two turboshaft engines, the Lear Fan was a summing-up of everything Lear had done. It carried many of his avionics inventions and had the stunning Lear-trademark elegance. The plane was built almost entirely of carbon-fiber composites including boron, fiberglass, Kevlar, and various resins, and its projected fuel economy and the quietness of its engines were in tune with mid-seventies concerns over the oil embargo and the environment. The Lear Fan was designed to fly at 400 miles per hour on one-fifth the fuel of a jet and was initially priced at $1.4 million. It promised a new era in fast, economical executive transport and pioneered new-materials technology that has since been applied to such planes as the McDonnell Douglas F/A-18 Hornet fighter and the record-breaking, around-the-world *Voyager*.

By the time the Lear Fan was taking its exotic shape, Bill Lear had nearly worn himself out with a life of brilliant creation. Four major medical operations in three years, one of them on his brain, had sapped his once unbelievable vitality. He had had four wives and six children; had invented car and airplane radios, navigation aids, autopilots, and the eight-track tape; and had developed the hot-rod executive Learjet—families, ideas, and careers enough for half a dozen men.

Lear was a starter, not always a finisher, and went through at least four fortunes bringing his dreams to life, each project seemingly more ambitious than the last. Even his failures—automobile steam engines, for example, that he promised would clean up the environment and save fossil fuels—had a palpable grandeur to them. One of them, the Lear Fan, still holds us transfixed. As much a work of art as a piece of engineering, it retains a certain inevitability. Lear himself estimated that the plane was ten years ahead of its time.

Freud would have understood Bill Lear: alternately abused and worshiped by his domineering mother, he ran away to the U.S. Navy when he was a teenager to escape her. He learned telegraphy in the Navy, then went to work for Western Union. "As soon as I became the fastest operator they had, I quit," Lear told the author of a 1969 *Esquire* magazine profile titled "What Bill Lear Wants, Bill Lear Invents." "That's one of my cardinal rules of success. Quit a job the minute you master it. Get another job where you can learn something new."

The shape of things to come: Only three Lear Fans were built, but the design's aerodynamics and advanced composite materials have had a far-reaching influence.

Lear was a one-third owner of Motorola until 1932, when he sold his share in the company to Paul Galvin, for whom he had designed the first practical car radio. In 1934 Motorola made more than half the 780,000 car radios sold that year. But by then Lear was more interested in radios for airplanes. He had already gone through his first fortune and his second marriage; his eight-dollar-a-week room in Chicago was so small, Lear joked, that he had to hang his toothbrush in the hall.

World War II made Lear his second fortune. He became a kingpin of America's 50,000-plane-a-year manufacturing effort by perfecting the linkages to operate radial engine cooling flaps and flight control surfaces. But his weakness in production and quality control was exposed when Lear Inc. held up one of the most massive industrial production efforts in history by keeping hundreds of B-24 Liberators waiting for their engine cooling mechanisms. Though preoccupied at the time developing the best automatic pilot system in the world (it won the Collier Trophy in

The Lear Fan's turboshaft engines each drove a shaft leading to a common transmission. The engineering was sound, but the gearbox was a source of problems during flight testing.

1950), Lear was forced to look on while other companies got most of the military contracts because the armed services trusted their craftsmanship over his.

After the war he found himself working on entire airplanes. Upgrading his personal Lockheed Model 18 Lodestar led to the rebuilding and refitting of others, creating the first luxury executive Learstars, capable of flying 80mph faster than the originals. There was an element of arrogance in Lear's re-engineering of the Lodestar, it being an advanced transport when it was introduced before the war.

In 1957 he sold the rights to the Learstar concept to finance the development of the plane that would be known as the Learjet. Bill Lear was one of the first to see the market for a dedicated business jet—not a converted military utility plane, as many corporate jets were then, but a fast status symbol. He brought in the designer of two Grumman fighters, Gordon Israel, to refine his Learjet Model 23 design. The plane looked sporty, having been derived from a Swiss fighter-bomber, the P-16. (The P-16 failed to achieve production after two of the first four built crashed into Lake Constance, becoming known as "Swiss submarines.") Learjets, however, were not totally practical. They lacked headroom, and since Lear believed that providing plumbing would be an admission that trips in the jet might take too long, Learjets had no washrooms.

The Learjet first flew on October 7, 1963, in the hands of former Republic Aviation test pilot Henry Beaird. Model 23 received its certificate on July 31, 1964, and Lear presided over the company until late 1967, when he sold his interest to the Gates Rubber Company of Denver. After he left, sound management made a Lear inspiration into an industry. A backhanded compliment to the Model 23 was the use of a Lockheed U-2 spy plane by the National Aeronautics and Space Administration in April 1989 to break the Learjet's weight-class world records for time-to-climb and altitude. (The U-2 had routinely broken those records since its introduction in 1955 but did so in secret.) By early 1980 Gates had sold its thousandth Learjet—one of more than a quarter of all business jets ever built—and was rolling out a stretched version, the Longhorn 50, with both toilet facilities and increased headroom.

By the late 1960s Lear had exhausted a third fortune on the development of a larger business jet with up-to-date turbofan engines and a thicker, "supercritical" wing that offered more lift and more internal fuel capacity. He called this marriage the LearStar 600 and, when he came to a financial crunch, shopped the design around. A former General Dynamics subsidiary, Montreal's Canadair, was looking for a keynote project and had government money to spend on development. Canadair bought an option on the LearStar for $375,000, plus future royalties amounting to $7.2 million, after certification, for Lear. As always, though, Lear had trouble being anybody's partner. He removed himself from the plane's development in 1977, taking most of his royalties in advance to finance his next and final obsession, the Lear Fan. In Canadair's hands, with tens of millions in Canadian government financing, the LearStar became the Canadair Challenger business jet, which since has been stretched into the Canadair RJ, or Regional Jet airliner.

Lear had begun talking about building a super-efficient business airplane out of new materials in 1954, noting in a speech to the Society of Automotive Engineers some years later that the technology to build such a machine was still not at hand. The concept itself was not new. Lear's idea of housing two engines in a single aerodynamic shape dates back to the giant Dornier Do J flying boats of the early 1920s. A configuration with twin engines in the fuselage and a pusher prop appeared during World War II in an experimental medium bomber, the Douglas XB-42 "Mixmaster," so named for the pair of contrarotating props behind its tail, but was soon eclipsed by the introduction of jets.

Lear had himself nursed the idea of twin engines, buried in the rear of the fuselage and powering a single pusher propeller, ever since he had been injured in a crash in which the failure of a wing-mounted engine on a twin-engined aircraft had caused the plane to spin. Turboprops, or gas-turbine engines, developed during the 1950s, were small and powerful enough to be installed near the tails of small

transports. When the final ingredient, carbon fiber, or graphite composite materials, appeared, Bill Lear was preoccupied with the LearStar. These materials required years of research before reaching a state of development, where they were claimed to be about half the weight of aluminum construction yet twice as strong.

Richard Tracy was Lear's chief engineer on the LearStar project. Out of the blue one day in early 1976, Lear asked him "how much fuel and how long would it take to fly an airplane with six to eight passengers from Los Angeles to New York at 400mph, at 41,000 feet, in a twin-engine, propeller-driven pusher." Tracy calculated that with two 500-shaft-horsepower gas turbines the trip would take about six hours, at 12 statute miles per gallon. The subject continued to pop up every couple of weeks or so.

In *Stormy Genius,* author Richard Rashke tells the story of how, after Canadair finally rejected Lear's never-ending improvements to the LearStar, Tracy told his deputy, Rod Schapel, that "Bill's going to die if he doesn't get one last shot." Schapel was assigned to do preliminary design on a pusher at home, but he also worked on it at the Lear hangar in Reno on weekends. Despite recent brain surgery, Lear could not be kept away from the action. One Saturday he caught Schapel at his drawing board.

"What are you doing?" he asked.

"Working on an airplane. It's a prop."

"I don't want to see anything like that around here."

The following Saturday Lear again found Schapel at work on the same plane. This time Lear sounded less convincing, so Schapel told him, "This is your new airplane, Bill." "Bullshit!" Lear said.

Lear was a mercurial character who often fired his engineers on Fridays and wondered where they were on Mondays. He quickly changed his mind about the propeller-driven aircraft that had, after all, been his own idea. He worked on the Lear Fan until only days before his death at seventy-six. His last words were "Finish it!"

Two years later, after his widow, Moya, had inherited the Lear Fan and Bill's final instructions to "Finish it," his dying wish was coming true.

After Lear died in 1976 hundreds of workers on two continents, led by Moya, dedicated themselves to getting his final project into the air. Lear Fan Model 2100 used up $260 million, but it did fly. The date of its first flight was recorded as December 32, 1980, to conform with a deadline imposed by the British government, which had partly financed it as a program to create jobs in Northern Ireland.

In 1980, the 500-odd workers at Lear's Reno hangar pinned on Finish It! badges and worked round the clock. On Christmas Eve, dinner was served on the floor of the Reno hangar that housed the almost-completed Lear Fan 001. One shift worked on the plane while the other shift ate, and all sang carols together with Federal Aviation Authority inspectors and their British counterparts. Henry Beaird took off in the Lear Fan prototype on New Year's Day, 1981, and changed seats with Dennis Newton in the air, allowing Newton to land it.

The Lear Fan should have been mass-produced. Its downfall was the expense of building a production management team before the prototype was fully developed, in the opinion of L. J. Hart-Smith, a Douglas Aircraft Company composite-materials specialist who worked with Moya Lear's team to iron out some of the remaining bugs in the plane's carbon-graphite structure. There was also a durability problem in the transmission, where the power of two engines was combined to run the single propeller. Even with $50 million in British government money and $20 million in deposits on the nearly 300 Lear Fans ordered, plus a further Saudi Arabian investment, the company ran out of money.

The Lear Fan Company, as it was known by then, went out of business in 1985. In the end, Lear Fan 001 was lucky to survive. The bankruptcy receivers, based in Denver, had planned to test it to destruction. An appeal went out to the Museum of Flight's membership for the $40,000 required to buy the plane. The campaign raised $46,000, with the surplus going toward transporting the plane to Seattle.

Unique among the Museum's artifacts, the Lear Fan is more than just a piece of aviation history. It continues, in some respects, to be well ahead of its time: fast but fuel-efficient, it could be a prototype all over again.

Bill Lear's last creation runs up its Pratt & Whitney turboshafts during ground testing. It first flew "December 32, 1980," a date formulated to comply with an end-of-1980 financing deadline.

LEAR FAN MODEL 2100

Dimensions

Overall wingspan 39ft 4in

Overall length 39ft 7in

Height 11ft 6in

Engines

Two 850-shaft-horsepower Pratt & Whitney of Canada PT-6B-35F turboshafts, flat-rated at 650hp each

Weight

Empty 3,850lbs

Loaded 7,200lbs

Performance

Maximum speed (at 31,000ft) . . . . more than 400mph

Rate of climb 3,550ft/min

Service ceiling 41,000ft

Range (with 45-minute reserve) 2,300mi

Homebuilts

There are tens of thousands of people in the Northwest who know something about building airplanes. Judging by the workmanship in the dozen or so examples of homebuilt aircraft in the Museum of Flight's collection, many of these workers put down the tools of their trade at the end of the day only to pick up them up again in their own basements or garages.

Here are four examples of the fruits of their labors. It is difficult to imagine a wider variety of aircraft than these: an ultralight autogyro; a handsome five-seat, twin-engine utility plane; a modernized biplane with tricycle landing gear; and an easy-to-build personal sportster that can be flown with one or two wings, on floats or on wheels.

Homebuilt aircraft are licensed by the Federal Aviation Administration on an annual-renewal basis as amateur experimental aircraft. They are subject to strict limitations, including the requirement to inform control towers and passengers of the nature of the aircraft. The word "experimental," which by law appears near the cockpit of every homebuilt, is meant as a warning. But it also celebrates the ingenuity and hard work of many individuals who have committed themselves to designing and building aircraft with their own hands.

Not an airplane, not a helicopter, the gyrocopter is an autogyro with a pusher propeller for horizontal flight. The rotors rotate because of the forward motion, without direct power.

BENSEN B-8M GYROCOPTER

The sales literature for this homebuilt seems unbelievable: with fewer parts than a bicycle, assembled with bolts "like an Erector set," flown from an unenclosed seat with "unequalled 360-degree visibility in all directions," its maintenance requirements reduced to "those of a motor scooter," Igor B. Bensen's Gyrocopter is that dream machine of the early 1950s, the suburbanite's one-person commuter ship.

Not an airplane and not a helicopter—Bensen calls his flying machine a "whirlybird"—the Gyrocopter derives its forward motion from a flat four-cylinder engine driving a pusher propeller. Takeoff speed is 20 miles per hour; or it can take off vertically in a 20mph wind. Its rotor revolves as a result of aerodynamic forces, a process called autorotation. Even if the motor fails, the rotor continues to develop lift and can safely lower the aircraft to the ground. A glider version operates without power and can be converted to a powered Gyrocopter. *Sports Illustrated* called it a "flying motorcycle."

The Gyrocopter can be operated with wheels, floats, or skids. Kits for critical components such as the rotor blades are available from the Bensen Aircraft Corporation in Raleigh, North Carolina, which claims that thousands of powered Gyros and gliders have been built. Karol Sowinski of Kent, Washingon, built and registered this one in 1982 and donated it to the Museum of Flight in 1986.

BENSEN B-8M GYROCOPTER

Dimensions

Height	5ft 10in
Length (less rotor)	11ft 3in
Rotor diameter	20ft

Engine

One McCulloch 4318A 4-cylinder horizontally opposed air-cooled 2-stroke engine, 90hp at 4,000rpm

Weight

Empty	235lbs
Maximum gross weight	500lbs
Useful load (including pilot)	270lbs

Performance

Takeoff speed	20mph
Maximum economy speed	45mph
Maximum speed	85mph
Landing speed	7mph
Range	100mi
Service ceiling	12,500ft

DURAND MARK V

Bill Durand of Omaha, Nebraska, designed his first airplane in 1934. Since then he has produced four more original aircraft, including a monoplane pusher intended for mass production in 1948 that fell victim to the postwar collapse of the general aircraft industry. Oddly enough, Durand's first four designs were monoplanes; only during the late 1960s did he get around to conceiving a biplane, the Mark V.

The Mark V represents everything Durand had learned. He says his design philosophy was "adapting the machine to its builder-pilot and his passengers instead of making them conform to the machine.... I have rated gentle flying characteristics, short field capability, personal comfort, cross-country usefulness, occupant safety, and structural simplicity more important than extremely light weight, high cruising speed, or other strictly competitive numbers."

The Durand biplane has negative stagger—the lower wing is set ahead of the upper—for spinproof, low-speed flying characteristics. The windshield pushes forward with the doors for easy, car-type entry, and the plane offers the pilot near-panoramic visibility with a rear window. Ground handling is improved by its nosewheel landing gear and full-span flaps on both wings.

Making the Mark V a biplane allowed Durand to endow it with compact dimensions: he claims the prototype was built on a 4-by-8ft plywood table in a 14-by-15ft shop that also housed a workbench, drill press, stove, restroom, and the library of his local chapter of the Experimental Aircraft Association! The Durand's all-metal, pop-riveted construction eliminates glue fumes and has the additional benefit of resulting in a factory-built appearance. The prototype flew June 28, 1978.

It took John P. Foy of Bellevue, Washington, one month less than five years—2,500 hours—and $25,500 to build 444JF after starting in April 1979. The Durand was his fourth homebuilt project. He used rebuilt powerplant components and lavished a professional paint job on the plane. It was donated to the Museum of Flight, in "perfect flying condition," in time for the opening of the Museum's Great Gallery in July 1987. Foy was quite happy with the Durand's leisurely cruise speed of 115mph; he has logged all the serious, high-speed flying hours he needs piloting 747s across the Pacific.

DURAND MARK V

Dimensions

Overall wingspan	24ft 6in
Length	20ft 3in
Height	6ft 5in

Engine

One Lycoming O320, 160hp at 2,700rpm

Weight

Empty	1,189lbs
Design gross weight	1,840lbs

Performance

Maximum speed	170mph
Cruising speed	115mph
Liftoff	62–70mph
Approach	80mph

Fly Baby is "an easy-to-build, easy-to-fly, low-cost folding-wing airplane that can be towed or trailered from the airport for storage in a standard-sized home garage," *The Encyclopedia of Homebuilt Aircraft* says. "The Fly Baby is what you might call a home builder's homebuilt."

Peter M. Bowers won the one and only competition to design such a handyman's dream. Sponsored in 1962 by the Experimental Aircraft Association, the national organization of home airplane builders, the contest resulted in a remarkable aircraft by any standard.

The Fly Baby can be operated as a monoplane or biplane, on wheels or on floats. It can cruise slightly longer than three hours on twelve to sixteen gallons of fuel and is unusually aerobatic for a 65-horsepower airplane. Owners have modified their Fly Babys with cockpit canopies, racy wheel spats, and streamlined cowlings.

Best of all, Bowers estimates that his plane can be built, without specialized tools, jigs, or materials, in the equivalent of two hours per day—plus all day Saturday—for one year. The basic material is wood, and the construction methods can be compared to those for an oversized model airplane.

Rather than presenting his plans in the usual blueprint form, Bowers wrote the Fly Baby's building instructions in a 200-page book. The detailed written instructions eliminate guesswork and are accompanied by drawings of ribs and metal fittings. Bowers also includes chapters on flight testing and FAA requirements and paperwork.

The Museum of Flight, of which Bowers is a charter member, has Fly Baby N4339. It took Al Stabler of Allyn, Washington, about twenty months to build it, from the start of construction in February 1968 to final cover, with nine coats of dope, on September 1, 1970. Stabler flew it 130-odd hours over ten years ending in 1980, and donated it to the Museum in 1986.

Perhaps the best testimonial to its docile flying characteristics, Bowers says, is the fact that 285 different pilots, some with as little as thirty-five flying hours and others with no experience at all in small airplanes, had flown the prototype Fly Baby up to December 1989. As of that date, over 400 Fly Babys had been built.

It can fly with one wing or two, with wheels or floats, hands on or off, open cockpit or enclosed, and it can be built, Bowers says, "by anyone capable of getting good grades in a high school wood-shop course."

BOWERS FLY BABY

Dimensions

Overall wingspan 28ft

Overall length . . . . 18ft 10 ½in

Height (folded) 6ft 11in

Engine

Any standard 65–85hp aircraft engine. Bowers recommends not exceeding 85hp or using electric starters. N4339 has a 65hp Continental A65-8.

Weight

Empty 605lbs

Loaded 925lbs

Performance

Cruising speed (depending on engine) 95–115mph

Rate of climb 850–1,100ft/min

The Wickham Model B is the product of a lifetime of flight-related activity by James Wickham, an aerodynamicist at Boeing for thirty-five years (who, incidentally, soloed on his first flight). A graduate of the Massachusetts Institute of Technology and former chief of aerodynamics at Boeing Wichita, Wickham was, in his own words, involved in a lot of oddball projects during an active career that included work on the nuclear-powered B-52 study. Wickham didn't make the big Model B from a kit; he designed and built it from scratch, taking more than ten years from start to finish.

The Model B amounts to a fully engineered, factory-built, all-metal, five-place twin-engine airplane—of which only one was made. The factory may have been Wickham's basement, but it was a basement designed to accommodate a 40ft wing under construction: Wickham handed his architect the plans for the Model B and instructed him to build his new house around it.

There have been five Wickham plane designs. (A sixth, the Model F, was being worked on during the late 1980s.) The Model E was a tiny all-wood, Volkswagen-powered single-seater that was, Wickham says, "such a nice-feeling airplane that you hated to stop flying it." It first flew in August 1979 and, despite its flying qualities, had only seven hours on it after almost a year. Wickham decided to sell it, but before doing so, "I decided to check the spin characteristic before selling it to some inexperienced soul who might kill himself in it." Instead, it was Wickham who came close to missing his 68th birthday, which was only days away, when he was unable to recover the Model E from its spin:

"I felt like a mouse riding one of those old-fashioned ceiling fans that were in restaurants and public buildings fifty years ago." He bailed out, landed hard, and awoke to find himself being licked by a friendly cow.

Why is the Model B a twin? "The tall trees and rugged country of the Pacific Northwest provide very few places suitable for a forced landing. The country scared me and I decided that I needed a twin-engine airplane."

Even with two engines, the hallmark of the Model B is its simplicity. It has no fuel pumps to fail, no hydraulic system to leak, no gear retraction or variable-pitch propellers to go wrong.

"The airplane is stable about all three axes and is very easy to fly," Wickham writes in his handwritten "Design, Construction and Flight Notes," backing his testimonial with a total of 635 hours' flight time on the Model B. These notes are full of Wickham's droll, self-deprecating sense of humor. At medium weight, he writes, the Wickham will fly on one engine, with the other prop windmilling, but "at gross weight the single-engine ceiling is near sea level." Lose an engine at heavy weight, and "you should expect to land in the not-too-distant future."

After a lengthy design period that included construction of a full-scale cabin mock-up, fabrication started around Christmas 1957 with cutting and assembly of the control-surface trim tabs. It cost $17,500 in materials to build. The plane first flew in April 1968, and Wickham donated it to the Museum of Flight in March 1986. "Well," he says now, "it was a lot of work. You'd have to be an idiot to even start."

"Why a twin? The tall trees and rugged country of the Pacific Northwest provide very few places suitable for a forced landing." Jim Wickham, Boeing engineer, 1966. So he built himself an all-metal, twin-engine airplane.

WICKHAM MODEL B

Dimensions

Overall wingspan 40ft 3in

Length 25ft 10in

Height 9ft 10in

Engines

Two Lycoming O-290-Ds, 150hp each

Weight

Empty 1,900lbs

Loaded 3,000lbs

Useful load 1,100lbs

Seats 4–5

Performance

Maximum speed 150mph

Cruise (low power setting) 100–120mph

Rate of climb (loaded) 1,500ft/min

Range 500mi

Glossary

This glossary is limited to the references in the text.

Aerobatics: A contraction of the term ''air acrobatics.'' Aircraft maneuvers such as loops, rolls, and wingovers.

Aerodynamics: The science that deals with the movement of bodies through air and other gaseous fluids, and the forces that act upon those bodies.

Afterburner: A system that augments power or thrust from a jet engine by burning additional fuel mixed with unused oxygen from the engine's exhaust.

Aileron: A hinged, movable surface, usually on the outer trailing edge of an aircraft's wings, controlling the rolling or banking movements of the aircraft.

Aircraft: The term ''aircraft'' has come to mean heavier-than-air flying machines, to the exclusion of balloons, dirigibles, and gliders.

Airframe: The basic structure of an aircraft. Everything but the engines and the avionics.

Airplane: A heavier-than-air aircraft, driven by an engine, that obtains lifting force from the effect of air flowing against its wings.

Angle of Attack: The acute angle between the line of the normal wind direction and the chord of an airfoil. (The chord is a line connecting an airfoil profile at two points, the leading and trailing edges.)

Area Rule: A design concept controlling the cross-sectional area of an aircraft along its length, for the purpose of avoiding large, abrupt changes (at the cockpit canopy or the wings, for instance), which incur severe drag penalties at speeds nearing the speed of sound.

Attack Plane: An airplane designed and equipped primarily for low-flying bombing or strafing attacks.

Avionics: The electrical and electronic devices and systems used in aircraft.

Barnstorming: The use of airplanes for taking passengers on joyrides, performing exhibition flying, etc.

Biplane: An airplane with wings on two different levels, especially one above and one below the fuselage.

Chandelle: A sudden steep, climbing turn of an airplane, simultaneously changing flight direction and gaining altitude.

Control Surface: Any movable airfoil used to guide or control an aircraft in the air, including the rudder, elevators, ailerons, spoiler flaps, trim tabs, and the like.

Cowling: A removable cover placed over part of an aircraft, especially an engine.

Drag: A retarding force acting upon an aircraft that exerts itself parallel to the direction of motion of the aircraft.

Elevator: A control surface normally on the trailing edge of the horizontal stabilizer that, when deflected, makes the aircraft's nose go up or down.

Empennage: The tail assembly at the rear end of an aircraft, comprising the horizontal and vertical stabilizers and their associated control surfaces.

Fillet: A concave fairing to smooth out a surface area or junction between airframe parts, such as where the wing joins the fuselage, to facilitate airflow and reduce drag.

Flap: A hinged, movable section of the trailing edge of a wing that is extended into the airstream to increase lift during takeoff or drag during landing.

Fowler Flap: A kind of flap set into a wing, which moves backward and swings downward, used to increase the lift with a minimum amount of drag. Named after Harlan D. Fowler, American aeronautical engineer.

Fuselage: The main structure or central section of an airplane, which houses or contains the crew, passengers, cargo, etc.; the body or hull of an airplane.

Ground Loop: A violent turn of an airplane while taxiing, or during a landing or takeoff run.

High-Lift Device: A flap, slot, slat, or boundary-layer device that increases the lift of a wing.

Horsepower: A unit of power used in measuring an engine's output, equal to the power required to lift 33,000 pounds one foot in one minute.

Intercooler: A radiator, usually placed directly in the airstream, used to dissipate heat from either engine coolant or oil and return it to the engine.

Jet Engine: An engine that takes in air from outside for use as a fuel oxidizer and projects a jet of hot gases backward to create thrust, the gases being produced by combustion within the engine. (See also turboprop, turbofan.)

Mach Number: A number expressing the ratio of the speed of a moving body (or a part thereof) through the air, to the speed of sound in the air. The speed of sound varies with altitude: at sea level it is 762mph. It declines with increasing altitude and is 658mph at 36,000ft. Mach 1.0 indicates a velocity equal to the speed of sound, 0.5 half the speed of sound, etc. Named for Ernst Mach, an Austrian physicist.

Monocoque: A structure, usually curved or oval in cross section, whose primary stresses are borne by the outer skin rather than by any internal stiffening members. An example in nature is the eggshell.

Monoplane: An airplane with only one pair of wings.

Nacelle: A separate, streamlined enclosure on an airplane for sheltering or housing something, such as an engine.

Power, Military Rated: The maximum thrust or power an engine can develop without damage for a period of time specified by qualified authority.

Power, Normal Rated: The maximum power an engine can develop continuously for an extended period of time without damage, as specified by qualified authority.

Powerplant: The engine and all systems required to make it run, including supporting structures, air induction, fuel, cooling, and ignition systems.

Powertrain: The mechanism by which power is transmitted from an engine to a propeller or axle that it drives.

Propwash: The backwash of air produced by a propeller.

Pursuit Plane: A fighter airplane designed primarily for pursuit of and attack on enemy aircraft.

Ramjet: A jet engine with no moving parts. Since it is basically a cylinder with burners inside, it requires the motion of air through it to work.

Radial Engine: An air-cooled internal combustion engine in which the stationary cylinders radiate from a common crankcase.

Rudder: A vertically oriented control surface that, when deflected, makes the aircraft rotate about its vertical axis.

Slat: A long, usually narrow auxiliary airfoil.

Spin: A controlled or uncontrolled maneuver in which an aircraft falls in a helical path, usually entered into while flying at an angle of attack greater than the angle of maximum lift.

Spinner: A rounded or cone-shaped streamlined fairing fitted over the hub of an aircraft propeller, which rotates with the propeller.

Stall: The action of an airplane when, by the separation of the airflow, as in the case of insufficient airspeed or of an excessive angle of attack, the airplane tends to drop.

Static Thrust: Thrust without motion, as when a jet engine is tested at rest. The unit of measurement of jet engine power is pounds of static thrust (pst).

Test Bed: An aircraft used to test various engine configurations in flight.

Test Stand: A stationary stand on which an aircraft engine is tested or its thrust is measured.

Trim Tab: A small auxiliary plate or airfoil in the trailing edge of a control surface that can be adjusted to assist in moving the larger surface.

Turbofan, Fanjet, or Bypass Engine: A development of the turbojet in which a ducted (cowled) fan ahead of the intake and larger in diameter than the compressor blades drives much of the air intake past the compressor blades, thus bypassing the rest of the engine.

The fan thus generates additional thrust with very little additional fuel use. Advantages of the turbofan are fuel economy, better performance at low altitudes, and noise reduction due to the shielding of the hot exhaust gases within a cylindrical stream of cooler air, reducing the characteristic jet-engine noise created by hot gases hitting the cold atmosphere.

Turboprop, Turboshaft Engine: A jet engine designed to drive a propeller from the turbine shaft.

Wheel Bogie: A single landing-gear strut carrying two, four, or more wheels. A Boeing 747's main landing gear bogies carry four wheels apiece.

Wing Root: The base of an airplane's wing, where it joins and is faired into the fuselage.

Yaw: The movement of an aircraft about its vertical axis.

This glossary is adapted from several sources, including:

The Compact Edition of the Oxford English Dictionary. New York: Oxford University Press, 1971.

Heflin, Woodford Agee, ed. *The United States Air Force Dictionary.* Washington, DC: Air University Press, 1956.

Heinemann, Edward H., Rosario Rausa, and K. E. Van Every. *Aircraft Design.* Baltimore: Nautical & Aviation, 1985.

Taylor, John W. R., ed. *The Lore of Flight.* New York: Crescent Books, 1986.

Wragg, David W., comp. *A Dictionary of Aviation.* New York: Frederick Fell Publishers, 1974.

Bibliography

AVIATION AND AIRCRAFT DESIGN IN GENERAL

Boyne, Walter J. *The Smithsonian Book of Flight*. Washington, DC: Smithsonian Books, 1987.

Boyne flew B-47s, is a former director of the National Air and Space Museum, and has produced the best general-interest history of flight currently in print.

Gilbert, James. *The Great Planes*. New York: Grosset & Dunlap, 1970.

Out of print. Includes brightly written profiles of seven types in the Museum of Flight collection.

Gunston, Bill. *The Anatomy of Aircraft*. London: Brian Trodd, 1988.

A fine companion book: developmental histories of fifty-four types of aircraft, six of which are in this book.

Hallion, Richard. *Test Pilots: The Frontiersmen of Flight*. rev. ed. Washington, DC: Smithsonian Institution Press, 1988.

An absorbing history of flight from the point of view of test pilots and engineers.

Heinemann, Edward H., Rosario Rausa, and K. E. Van Every. *Aircraft Design*. Baltimore: Nautical & Aviation, 1985.

Heinemann, designer of the A-4 Skyhawk, designs a mythical attack jet. Fine glossary.

Oakes, Claudia M., and Kathleen L. Brooks-Pazmany. *Aircraft of the National Air and Space Museum*. Washington, DC: Smithsonian Institution Press, 1985.

Editors of Time-Life Books, and various authors. The Epic of Flight (series). Alexandria, VA: Time-Life Books, 1980–1984.

Individual titles appear in the bibliographies for specific aircraft models below.

ON BOEING

Bowers, Peter M. *Boeing Aircraft Since 1916*. Annapolis, MD: Naval Institute Press, 1989.

New edition of the definitive Boeing history, with new chapters on the 747 through 767 models.

Cleveland, Carl M. *Boeing Trivia*. Seattle: CMC Books, 1989.

Company stories and anecdotes by the man who succeeded Harold Mansfield as PR director of the Boeing Company.

Ingells, Douglas J. *747: The Story of the Boeing Super Jet*. Fallbrook, CA: Aero Publishers, 1970.

Mansfield, Harold. *Vision: A Saga of the Sky*. Salem, NH: Ayer Publishing, 1979.

A very readable history of the Boeing Company up to the design of the 707, by a company executive. Recently reprinted and available in paperback.

Redding, Robert, and Bill Yenne. *Boeing: Planemaker to the World*. New York: Crescent Books, 1983.

CURTISS JENNY

Bowers, Peter M. *Curtiss Aircraft 1907–1947*. Annapolis, MD: Naval Institute Press, 1987.

Curtiss Aeroplane and Motor Corporation. *The Curtiss Standard JN-4D Military Tractor Handbook, 1918*. Reprint. Appleton, WI: Aviation Publications, 1971.

Gilbert, James. *The Great Planes*. New York: Grosset & Dunlap, 1970.

Jerram, Michael F. *Antiques of the Air*. London: New English Library, 1980.

Kilduff, Peter. "Curtiss Jenny." In *Flying the World's Great Aircraft*, edited by Anthony Robinson. New York: Crescent Books, 1982.

Klym, Julie Opel. "Paper Planes." *Air Classics*, March 1981.

Milberry, Larry. *Aviation in Canada*. Toronto: McGraw-Hill, 1979.

O'Neil, Paul. *Barnstormers and Speed Kings*. The Epic of Flight. Alexandria, VA: Time-Life Books, 1981.

Prendergast, Curtis. *The First Aviators*. The Epic of Flight. Alexandria, VA: Time-Life Books, 1981.

Tallman, Frank. *Flying the Old Planes*. New York: Doubleday, 1973.

BOEING P-12

Aeronautical staff of Aero Publishers Inc., with Edward T. Maloney. *Boeing P-12, F4B*. Aero Series, no. 5. Fallbrook, CA: Aero Publishers, 1966.

Cleveland, Carl M. "The Oldest Boeing Still Flying." *Air Classics*, December 1978.

Editors of *Flying* magazine. *The Best of Flying: A Fifty-Year Sampler*. New York: Van Nostrand, Reinhold, 1977. See Eaker, "Alone Across America—BLIND!" May 1938; Miller, "Paul Mantz, A Pilot's Pilot," July 1962; Morrison, "A Movie Magnate's Racer," August 1937.

Wallick, S. L. "Lew," Jr., and Peter M. Bowers. *Flying the P-12*. Seattle: Museum of Flight, 1982.

BOEING 80A

Bowers, Peter M. *Flying the Boeing Model 80*. Seattle: Museum of Flight, 1984.

Day, Beth. *Glacier Pilot: The Story of Bob Reeve and the Men Who Pushed Back the Arctic Frontier*. New York: Henry Holt, 1957.

Feeny, Bill. "Famous Alaska Bush Pilots." *Air Classics 1978 Yearbook*, 1978.

Stroud, John. "Comfort in the Air." In *Air Transport Before the Second World War*, edited by John W. R. Taylor and Kenneth Munson. London: New English Library, 1975.

AERONCA C-2

Bowers, Peter M. "Of Wings and Things." *The Western Flyer*, September 1988.

Matt, Paul R. "Aeronca: Its Formation and First Aircraft." *Historical Aviation Album*. Temple City, CA: Paul R. Matt, 1971.

Spenser, Jay P. *Aeronca C-2: The Story of the Flying Bathtub*. Washington, DC: Smithsonian Institution Press, 1978.

STEARMAN PT-13A KAYDET AND C-3B

Bowers, Peter M., and Mitch Mayborn. *Stearman Guidebook*. 2d ed. Dallas: Flying Enterprise Publications, 1972.

Davisson, Budd. "Stearman: The Legend Lives On." *Vintage Aircraft Buyer's Guide and Price Digest*, Summer 1989.

Jerram, Michael F. *Antiques of the Air*. London: New English Library, 1980.

Johnson, Robert S., and Martin Caidin. *Thunderbolt!* New York: Ballantine Books, 1958.

BOEING 247D

Coleman, Theodore, with Robert Wenkam. *Jack Northrop and the Flying Wing: The Real Story Behind the Stealth Bomber*. New York: Paragon House, 1988.

Green, William, and Gordon Swanborough. *The World's Great Fighter Aircraft*. London: Salamander Books, 1981.

Seely, Victor D. "Boeing's Pacesetting 247." *American Aviation Historical Society Journal*, Winter 1964: 239–71.

DOUGLAS DC-3

Bowers, Peter M. *The DC-3: 50 Years of Legendary Flight*. Blue Ridge Summit, PA: TAB Books, 1986.

Francillon, René J. *McDonnell Douglas Aircraft Since 1920*. London: Putnam, 1979.

Ingells, Douglas J. *The Plane that Changed the World: A Biography of the DC-3*. Fallbrook, CA: Aero Publishers, 1966.

Morgan, Len. *The Douglas DC-3*. Famous Aircraft Series. Fallbrook, CA: Aero Publishers, 1980.

O'Leary, Michael. "Dakota Stand-Down." *Air Classics*, June 1989.

O'Leary, Michael. "North America's Last Military C-47 Squadron." *Air Classics*, September 1988.

Pearcy, Arthur. "Douglas Commercial Two." *Air Enthusiast* 19, 1982.

BOEING B-17F FLYING FORTRESS

Bendiner, Elmer. *The Fall of Fortresses: A Personal Account of the Most Daring, and Deadly, American Air Battles of WWII*. New York: Putnam, 1980.

Bowers, Peter M. *50th Anniversary, Boeing Flying Fortress, 1935–1985*. Seattle: Museum of Flight, 1985.

Caidin, Martin. *Flying Forts*. New York: Ballantine Books, 1968.

Collison, Thomas. *Flying Fortress: The Story of the Boeing Bomber*. New York: Scribner, 1943.

Green, William. *Famous Bombers of the Second World War*, vol. 1. Garden City, NJ: Doubleday, 1969.

Freeman, Roger A., and Rikyu Watanabe. *B-17 Flying Fortress*. London: Jane's, 1983.

Jablonski, Edward. *Flying Fortress: The Illustrated Biography of the B-17s and the Men Who Flew Them*. New York: Doubleday, 1965.

O'Leary, Michael, ed. *Flying Fortress: An Air Combat Special*. Canoga Park, CA: Challenge Publications, 1985.

Willmott, H. P. *B-17 Flying Fortress*. London: Bison Books, 1980.

GENERAL MOTORS FM-2 WILDCAT

Green, William. *Famous Fighters of the Second World War*. 2d rev. ed., New York: Doubleday, 1975.

Gunston, Bill. *Grumman: Sixty Years of Excellence*. New York: Orion Books, 1988.

Kinzey, Bert. *Detail and Scale: F4F Wildcat*. Detail and Scale Series, vol. 30. Blue Ridge Summit, PA: TAB Books, 1988.

Linn, Don. *F4F Wildcat in Action*. Carrollton, TX: Squadron/Signal Publications, 1988.

Maas, Jim. *F2A Buffalo in Action*. Carrollton, TX: Squadron/Signal Publications, 1987.

O'Leary, Michael. *United States Naval Fighters of World War II in Action*. London: Blandford Press, 1980.

Sakai, Saburo, with Martin Caidin, and Fred Saito. *Samurai!* New York: Doubleday, 1978.

Thruelson, Richard. *The Grumman Story*. New York: Praeger, 1976.

GOODYEAR FG-1 CORSAIR

Henderson, Brian. "Out of the Deeps." *Air Progress Warbirds International*, Spring 1985.

Houser, William D. "Vought F4U Corsair." In *Flying the World's Great Aircraft*, edited by Anthony Robinson. New York: Crescent Books, 1982.

Johnsen, Frederick A., and Rikyu Watanabe, *F4U Corsair*. London: Jane's, 1983.

Lindbergh, Charles A. "Thoughts of a Combat Pilot." *Saturday Evening Post*, 2 October 1954.

Tallman, Frank. *Flying the Old Planes*. New York: Doubleday, 1973.

BOEING B-47E STRATOJET

Boyne, Walter J. "Bomber 47." *Wings* (US), August 1981.

Hallion, Richard P. *Designers and Test Pilots*. The Epic of Flight. Alexandria, VA: Time-Life Books, 1983.

Ingells, Douglas J. *747: The Story of the Boeing Super Jet*. Fallbrook, CA: Aero Publishers, 1970.

Peacock, Lindsay. *Boeing B-47 Stratojet*. Osprey Air Combat Series. London: Osprey, 1987.

Von Kármán, Theodor, and Lee Edson. *The Wind and Beyond*. Boston: Little, Brown, 1967.

HILLER YH-32 HORNET HELICOPTER

Christy, Joe, and Page Shamburger. *Summon the Stars: The Advance of Aviation from the Second World War*. Cranbury, NJ: A. S. Barnes, 1970.

Flynn, William. "The Hiller-Copter: Teen-age Inventor Constructs Helicopter with Twin Rotors and Simplified Controls." *Flying*, December 1944.

Gunston, Bill. *The Planemakers*. London: New English Library, 1980.

Holm, Harvey. "Design of the Hiller HJ-1, YH-32 Helicopter." *Aeronautical Engineering Review*. October 1953: 48–53.

Mikesh, Robert C. "Hiller XH-44 Hiller-Copter." In *Aircraft of the National Air and Space Museum*, edited by Claudia M. Oakes and Kathleen L. Brooks-Pazmany. Washington, DC: Smithsonian Institution Press, 1985.

Polmar, Norman, and Floyd D. Kennedy Jr. *Military Helicopters of the World*. Annapolis, MD: Naval Institute Press, 1981.

Taylor, John W. R., and Gordon Swanborough. *Military Aircraft of the World*. New York: Scribner, 1975.

Young, Warren R. *The Helicopters*. The Epic of Flight. Alexandria, VA: Time-Life Books, 1982.

DOUGLAS A-4 SKYHAWK II

Braybrook, Roy. "A-4 Skyhawk: A Long-Lasting Lightweight of Exaggerated Excellence?" *Air International*, November 1981.

Chesneau, Roger. *Skyhawk: McDonnell Douglas A-4M Skyhawk*. Aeroguide Series. Ongar, Essex: Linewrights, 1986.

Francillon, René J. *McDonnell Douglas Aircraft Since 1920*. London: Putnam, 1979.

Gunston, Bill. *Attack Aircraft of the West*. New York: Scribner, 1974.

Heinemann, Edward H., Rosario Rausa, and K. E. Van Every. *Aircraft Design*. Baltimore: Nautical & Aviation, 1985.

Heinemann, Edward H., and Rosario Rausa. *Ed Heinemann, Aircraft Designer*. Annapolis, MD: Naval Institute Press, 1980.

Kilduff, Peter. "Douglas A-4 Skyhawk." In *Flying the World's Great Aircraft*, edited by Anthony Robinson. New York: Crescent Books, 1982.

Rausa, Rosario. *Skyraider: The Douglas A-1 "Flying Dump Truck."* Baltimore: Nautical & Aviation, 1982.

Tegler, John. "Skyhawks for the Angels." *Air Classics Quarterly Review*, Spring 1979.

CHANCE VOUGHT XF8U-1 CRUSADER

Anderton, David A. "Vought's Crusader Design Meets Navy's High-Performance Criteria." *Aviation Week*, 23 January 1956.

Bulban, Edwin J. "Afterburner Pushes F8U-1P to Trans-U.S. Speed Mark." *Aviation Week*, 22 July 1957.

"Crusader, Last of the Gunfighters." *The Illustrated Encyclopedia of Aircraft,* edited by Stan Morse, vol. 13, no. 151, 1984.

Gunston, Bill. "Crusader: An Analysis of Chance Vought's Supersonic Naval Fighter." *Flight,* 24 May 1957.

Gunston, Bill. *Early Supersonic Fighters of the West.* London: Ian Allen, 1976.

Joos, Gerhard. *The Chance Vought F8A-E Crusader.* Surrey, England: Profile Publications, 1966.

Kinzey, Bert. *Detail and Scale: F-8 Crusader.* Detail and Scale Series, no. 31. Blue Ridge Summit, PA: TAB Books, 1988.

Mersky, Peter. "Vought's Long-Lived Photo Bird." *Air International,* September 1987.

APOLLO COMMAND MODULE

Armstrong, Neil, Michael Collins, and Edwin E. Aldrin Jr., with Gene Farmer and Dora Jane Hamblin. *First on the Moon.* Boston: Little, Brown, 1970.

Brooks, Courtney G., James M. Grimwood, and Lloyd S. Swenson Jr. *Chariots for Apollo: A History of Manned Lunar Spacecraft.* Washington, DC: National Aeronautics and Space Administration, 1979.

Collins, Michael. *Carrying the Fire: An Astronaut's Journeys.* New York: Farrar, Straus & Giroux, 1989.

Collins, Michael. *Liftoff: The Story of America's Adventure in Space.* New York: Grove Press, 1988.

Gatland, Kenneth, et al. *The Illustrated Encyclopedia of Space Technology.* London: Salamander Books, 1981.

Goldberg, Jeff. "Lunar Reflections: The Apollo Astronauts Reminisce." *Omni,* July 1989.

Kelley, Kevin W., ed. *The Home Planet.* Reading, MA: Addison-Wesley; Moscow: Mir Publishers, 1988.

Murray, Charles, and Catherine Bly Cox. *Apollo: The Race to the Moon.* New York: Simon & Schuster, 1989.

BOEING 747

Editors of *Air International.* "Big and Beautiful: A Premiere for the New 747." *Air International,* May 1988.

Boeing Commercial Airplane Company. *747 Product Overview.* Seattle: Boeing Commercial Airplane Company, 1989.

Davis, Lou. "Industry's Boldest Venture: The Boeing 747." *Air Transport World* (Special Report), February 1970.

"First Flight—Moment of Truth." *Boeing Everett Flyer,* 24 February 1969.

"Giant 747 Impressive During First Flight." *Boeing News,* 13 February 1969.

Gilchrist, Peter. *Boeing 747.* Modern Civil Aircraft, no. 4. London: Ian Allen, 1985.

Green, William, and Gordon Swanborough. *The Illustrated Encyclopedia of the World's Commercial Aircraft.* New York: Crescent Books, 1978.

Ingells, Douglas J. *747: The Story of the Boeing Super Jet.* Fallbrook, CA: Aero Publishers, 1970.

Newhouse, John. "The Aircraft Industry." *The New Yorker,* 14, 21, 28 June, 5 July 1982.

Pinkerton, W. Stewart, Jr. "Phasing In the 747: Getting Ready to Fly Huge New Jetliner Is a Painstaking Process." *The Wall Street Journal,* 1 December 1969.

RUTAN VARIVIGGEN

Editors of *Air International.* "Aircraft & Industry." *Air International,* December 1985.

Bernstein, Berton. "A Reporter at Large: The Last Plum." *The New Yorker,* 4 August 1986.

Downie, Don, and Julia Downie. *The Complete Guide to Rutan Aircraft.* 3d ed. Blue Ridge Summit, PA: TAB Books, 1987.

Rutan Aircraft Factory. *VariViggen Owner's Manual.* Mojave, CA, undated.

Yeager, Jeana, and Dick Rutan, with Phil Patton. *Voyager.* New York: Harper & Row, 1989.

LEAR FAN MODEL 2100

Editors of *Air International.* "One Thousand Learjets . . ." *Air International,* May 1980.

Green, William, and Gordon Swanborough. *The Illustrated Encyclopedia of the World's Commercial Aircraft.* New York: Crescent Books, 1978.

Hart-Smith, L. J. *Design and Development of the First LearFan All-Composite Aircraft.* Douglas Paper no. 8184. Long Beach, CA: McDonnell Douglas Aircraft Corp., 1989.

Pocock, Chris. "Swan Song for the Dragon Lady." *Air International,* August 1989.

Rashke, Richard. *Stormy Genius: The Life of Aviation's Maverick, Bill Lear.* Boston: Houghton Mifflin, 1985.

Shaw, David. "What Bill Lear Wants, Bill Lear Invents." *Esquire,* September 1969.

Index

Photo Credits

Cloud pictures by Art Rangno